ON THE STREET
HOW WE
Created the
Homeless

ON THE STREET

How We Created the Homeless

Barbara Murphy

Cover design by Doowah Design Inc.
Printed and bound in Canada

Published with the financial assistance of the Manitoba Arts Council and The Canada Council for the Arts.

Canadian Cataloguing in Publication Data

Murphy, Barbara
    On the street: how we created the homeless

Includes bibliographical references and index.
ISBN 1-896239-68-4

    1. Homelessness—Canada. I. Title

HV4509.M87 2000   362.5'0971   C00-901158-7

Don't turn away your face.
But for God's good grace,
You could be in their place…

Julian Moore, David Heneker, and
Monty Norman, *Irma La Douce.*

Acknowledgements

I want to acknowledge and thank many people from other disciplines, not my own, whose earlier research contributed to this project. These include researchers in the areas of urban history, urban geography, psychiatry, housing, and even anthropology and archaeology. All their contributions appear in the Bibliography but a special acknowledgement is in order.

Henry, a homeless Ottawa carpenter, created the appeal for help which appears on the cover. I came across his creation while walking on the Rideau Canal recreational path.

Fred Albers gave me a generous amount of his time and a valuable perspective on the home building industry and the rental market in Quebec. Don Johnston of the Canadian Home Builders' Association provided many helpful documents on the issues across Canada. Mary Jane Norris of the Department of Indian and Northern Affairs shared extensive research on migration and mobility patterns of Canadian registered Indians during the 1990s. Elizabeth Gyles, Joan Meyer, Elaine O'Connor, Hazel Hayles, and Anna Nicolle gave indispensable assistance with research on suburbanization and gentrification.

I am grateful for the excellent service given by staff of the National Library of Canada and the library at Carleton University. A special thank you is also due to Debbie Lyon who edited and advised on the final text.

Thank you also to Paul Murphy for research assistance and Kevin Murphy for editorial assistance and for their considerable personal support during the year.

Table of Contents

CHAPTER 1

Today's Urban Homeless

A considerable amount of competition among cities, some of it even friendly, is a reality of modern urbanized countries. Municipal governments looking to expand their tax base are enthusiastic promoters of their city's assets compared to those of their rivals. Ordinary citizens who may not be so preoccupied with operating revenues are still hometown boosters with out-of-town visitors and with friends, relatives, and complete strangers who have the misfortune to live somewhere else. The term "world-class city" has become the proudest boast of everyone connected with a city, from the civic government to the media to the general population. The very words imply competition and pride. Few urban residents want to make their home in anything less than a city that is world-class.

Yet we are reminded daily that our city, the city we think is world-class, is coming up short. When we walk down the main streets of Canada's major cities, we have an uncomfortable feeling that our pride may be misplaced. Within one city block four, five, or six of our fellow citizens, huddled against storefronts, ask us for spare change. They have no physical resemblance to the rest of us— shabby and ill-equipped for Canada's weather, most look twice their actual age. We try not to notice their outstretched ball caps, but we pass them block after block in *our* city that we boast about to our friends. And we begin to ask ourselves, is there anything world-class about this picture?

The sad truth is, if these adult waifs were not there, in plain view every day, we would not think about the homeless at all. These reminders on our main streets are only the tip of the iceberg. Many more are out of sight, unwilling to be objects of pity or contempt or curiosity, and still more are simply trying to find a place to stay warm.

How many homeless there are is not precisely known—estimating the number of homeless nationwide is a process full of pitfalls. If the focus is on the number who are literally homeless, that is, people who sleep in shelters provided for homeless people or in other places most of us do not consider dwellings,[1] the task is next to impossible. Census counts in most countries assume that everyone has an address, making the normal type of census of little use in estimating the number of homeless.

Three attempts have been made by US and Canadian officials to conduct other-than-normal censuses intended to catch people who do not own or rent dwelling places. (This definition of the target group should be further qualified. Owning or renting are not the only ways people have access to homes. Family or friends may give accommodation on a regular basis and, although those being accommodated may not own or rent, they obviously have a home and an address where someone, including a census enumerator, may reach them.)

In 1980 the US Census Bureau counted people staying in shelters in 16 cities and, in addition, attempted an enumeration of homeless people in bus depots, train stations, and all-night theatres. Not satisfied with the reliability of its findings, the bureau never widely publicized the results.

In 1990 the Census Bureau tried again, this time casting a wider (and better designed) net. On the evening of March 20 census takers counted people in emergency shelters across the country. Enumeration of people on the street took place between 2 a.m. and 4 a.m. March 21, while those in abandoned and boarded-up buildings were counted from 4 a.m. to 8 a.m. The street count included homeless people actually seen sleeping in bus or train stations, subway stations, airports, hospital emergency rooms, and other locations where they were known to seek shelter at night. By limiting the street count to the homeless who were visible, the Census Bureau admitted it likely missed those who were well-hidden or moving about. More confident of its methodology nonetheless, the bureau published the 1990 figures, estimating approximately 240,000 homeless in the US.

In Canada, for the 1991 census, enumerators attempted a count of the homeless in 16 Canadian cities. On the same day in each city, census takers interviewed people served at local soup kitchens to determine where they had spent the previous night. Unlike the 1990 US census, Canadian interviews did not extend to people outside the soup kitchens, the homeless in parks and back alleys, and under bridges and viaducts. By the mid-1990s Statistics Canada announced the findings of the homeless census would not be released because of the poor quality of the data.

To report that the published findings of the 1990 US census were controversial would be an understatement. The cities of Baltimore and San Francisco, the US Conference of Mayors, 15 advocacy organizations, and seven homeless people sued the Census Bureau, claiming it "arbitrarily limited" its tally of the homeless population. The suit maintained that the bureau deliberately set out to undercount the homeless and, as a result, to reduce the level of funding for programs benefitting the homeless. Among the places the census takers did not check, according to the suit, were on rooftops, under tarpaulins, inside cardboard structures, and in bushes, cars, and trash bins.

There have also been non-government estimates of the homeless in both countries, most fraught with their own difficulties of reliability. In particular, in using these estimates to give the public some idea of the magnitude of the homelessness issue, the media have not always made clear how the homeless were defined in each case. Since there is a clear connection between homelessness and poverty, the definition in some estimates is widened to include all those living in inadequate or substandard housing or those doubling up in accommodation. As a result, a wide range of definitions has created a wide range of estimates and considerable confusion for most of the general public who like to decide on the seriousness of any national issue by relating to how many are affected by it.

It is risky, therefore, and even foolhardy to make still another estimate of the number of Canada's homeless. Overestimating invites public cynicism; underestimating incurs the wrath of service agencies that rely on public funding. Yet precise estimating is impossible.

Despite this reality, any discussion of the homeless population must be prefaced with a rough estimate of its size. Using the most limiting definition of the homeless as those using emergency shelters and those sleeping in the street, a reasonable approach may be to stop making futile attempts to find every homeless person, hidden or otherwise, and instead to make use of facts already established through interviews with the homeless in many reliable research studies.

Interviews with thousands of people using emergency shelters and soup kitchens have revealed that the people we are trying to count have no established pattern to their sleeping arrangements. Although many sleep in emergency shelters frequently, they also sleep in public places or outdoors occasionally, and many report in interviews that sometimes friends or relatives take them in for the night.

Peter Rossi, a Chicago researcher, conducted the most statistically reliable and responsible study of the size of the "literally" homeless population taken in any city. His 1986 study of the Chicago homeless counted (on one night in the winter and one night in the fall) a sample of those using emergency shelters and those actually found on the streets, that is, in unconventional sleeping places like train and bus stations, airports, lobbies, and arcades. He found that for every person in an emergency shelter bed on the night of his fall season count, almost one-and-a-half as many more were on the streets. A 1984 study by the US Housing and Urban Development Department (HUD) was not far off, estimating this ratio to be one to 1.78. Both Rossi's and HUD's ratios indicate that US census takers indeed missed some of the less visible homeless on the street. Putting this together with the information from interviews that many of the homeless sleep on the occasional night with friends or relatives, the street count on any given non-winter night should be increased to include those temporarily indoors but still without homes. Rossi suggests that for every one shelter resident there are likely two "street" homeless.

The street-to-shelter ratio method of estimating a large group of people who cannot be found is no more or less reliable than methods that count (and sometimes miss counting) heads. It should be taken as a rough guide only. It does not attempt to address the numbers of very poor Canadians whose incomes force them to live in substandard housing with constant fear of eviction if their meager incomes should temporarily disappear. Nor does it address the growing number of poor who must spend up to 70 percent of their incomes on rent leaving very little for food, nor those doubling up in accommodation. These real problems are dealt with in more depth in other studies.[2] The street-to-shelter ratio method addresses only those who are literally without homes.

A Canadian Council on Social Development (CCSD) report of the late 1980s estimated the number of homeless in shelters to be approximately 11,000 on a given night. Using a street-to-shelter ratio of two to one, and accounting for growth in shelter occupants since the CCSD study, a very rough estimate can be made of 35,000 to 40,000 literally homeless Canadians on a given night. This may be somewhat lower than figures used by the media and homeless advocates—confining an estimate to a given night misses many who are homeless throughout the year—but surely the point is that 35,000 to 40,000 Canadians without homes is a startling number. Indeed it is a national tragedy. It has a certain amount of consistency with the roughly 350,000 homeless estimated by Rossi for the ten-times-larger United States. It means that in our world-class cities in Canada we could have up to 10,000 homeless in each of Montreal and Toronto, up to 5,000 in Vancouver, and anywhere from 1,000 to 2,000 in each of Edmonton, Calgary, Ottawa, Winnipeg, Hamilton, Halifax, Saskatoon and Regina..

More is known about the nature of the homeless population than about its size. The homeless of the 1980s and 1990s are younger than the traditional inhabitants of the old Bowery and skid row areas. Studies in the 1950s estimated the average age in those earlier neighbourhoods at close to 50. Today most of the homeless are in the middle and low thirties. And while the homeless of the past were usually concentrated in a small ghetto making up only a few blocks of the inner city, the new homeless of the '80s and '90s, less harassed by the police and more willing to be visible, are spread throughout the whole of downtown.

Today's homeless are still predominantly male, although women and children make up a growing proportion. A recent Toronto task force study found that 29 percent of those in Toronto emergency shelters were women. The 1990 US census count of the homeless both in shelters and on the street showed that women represented 30 percent of the homeless population. The fact that women were notably absent among the homeless of past decades but have today grown to 30 percent is not easily explained. Whether women are leaving violent situations or are simply family heads unable to find affordable rental accommodation, the new trend toward more women among the homeless may be another consequence of the predominance of females (58 percent) among Canadians living below the poverty line.

Public policies affecting the mentally ill also affect the composition of the homeless population. Estimates of homeless people with psychiatric problems range from 20 percent to 35 percent. Even though the process of closing down institutions for the mentally ill has been completed for almost two decades, one in four homeless has reportedly required psychiatric treatment at one time or another, very likely in psychiatric departments of local hospitals. Study interviews also show a third of the homeless with alcohol or drug abuse problems.

There is little comfort in knowing that urban homelessness is not confined to North America. By the 1980s cities in the European Community were experiencing growing numbers of homeless on their streets. In London alone, where living on the street is called "sleeping rough," an estimated 40,000 young people were already homeless by 1984. In Paris the traditional homeless, the *clochards*, have increasingly shared the streets with younger homeless who have gravitated to Paris from all over France. Most of the new younger homeless, called travellers by the police, are concentrated in the city core but many have drifted to the suburbs and some go south to Cannes and to the Riviera. In Frankfurt, Rome, Milan, and other European cities more and more of the poor are without housing and, among them, an expanding group of the mentally ill. Australians have also seen a growing number of people living on the streets. An estimated 40,000 are homeless in Australia, predominantly single males as in the US and Canada but with a growing proportion of single women and women with families.

While homelessness has also become an issue abroad, no other country has held Canada's dubious distinction of receiving the strongest rebuke ever from the United Nations for inaction on homelessness and other poverty issues. The criticism from the UN Committee on Economic, Social and Cultural Rights in 1998 claimed that Canada's failure to implement policies for its poor over the previous five years had "exacerbated poverty and homelessness among vulnerable groups during a time of strong economic growth and increasing affluence." News of the UN report came in December while the homeless were bracing themselves for another Canadian winter. They were no doubt relieved when they heard the federal government respond that the UN charges were based on outdated data.

In fairness to Canada, other developed countries have also come close to failing grades in their mixture of responses to homelessness, most of them falling short of addressing the root causes. In general, senior levels of government have seen homelessness as a city problem, and cities, in turn, have scrambled to find solutions. Sometimes they blame the homeless for their own plight, sometimes they show compassion, but at the city level the solutions are necessarily makeshift.

On the compassionate side, cities have poured an increasing amount of money into emergency shelters since the late 1970s. More recently many Canadian cities have established task forces in an effort to get beyond the crisis-driven responses of the past two decades. Edmonton, Toronto, and Ottawa have taken this step. Calgary established a homeless foundation funded by the public. In addition, in an attempt to force federal government action, the mayors and councils of Canada's ten largest cities passed resolutions in late 1998 declaring homelessness a national disaster.

On the not-so-compassionate side, many cities began to respond to a growing public irritation in the 1990s with the whole homelessness issue which was by then over 15 years old. New tougher attitudes first appeared in a handful of American cities in the form of by-laws restricting begging by the homeless. In some if not most cases, concern about the effect of panhandling on tourists was the real issue. Berkeley's by-law prohibited begging at night; Fort Lauderdale banned begging on beaches; New York banned it on subways and at subway stops. In Chicago the homeless were not allowed at the airport; in Santa Barbara they were not allowed to sleep on public streets. In Miami windshield washing was banned.

Further north in Florida, Orlando passed a by-law requiring panhandlers to register at police headquarters and wear a photo ID at all times. Panhandlers in Orlando were not allowed to beg at train and bus stops, automatic banking machines, and parks.

In Las Vegas police used existing trespassing laws to move the homeless out of sight of tourists. To clean up its image before the 1996 Olympics, Atlanta arrested beggars and swept the homeless out of vacant buildings and parking lots. New York City, in particular, went after the homeless on its streets under the direction of its new mayor, Rudolph Giuliani, who was elected in 1993. Panhandling was outlawed and windshield washing by young homeless, by now called squeegee kids, was banned.

Tougher attitudes also began to appear in Canadian cities in the 1990s. Elected officials, reflecting the growing impatience of the public, openly called the homeless "pests," "intimidators" and "thugs." Winnipeg was one of the first to turn harsher attitudes into legislation by passing a 1995 by-law to regulate begging by the homeless. Panhandling was banned near banks, automatic teller machines, hospitals, and bus stops, on buses, elevators, and pedestrian walkways. It was also illegal to panhandle from motorists at traffic lights. Those who violated the by-law could be fined up to $1,000, or given a prison term of up to six months.

Winnipeg's by-law became the general model introduced in Canadian cities throughout the remainder of the 1990s. An early by-law in Calgary was intended to ban begging on the Stephen Avenue and Barclay malls only, but later the ban was extended to bank entrances and bus stops and to all begging between 8 p.m. and 8 a.m. In Calgary the fine was $50.

New Westminster also passed a by-law outlawing panhandling near banks and bus stops, adding liquor store entrances as well. Within a few short weeks the number of panhandlers decreased. When asked by the media where they had gone, New Westminster's mayor replied that they had very likely gone to Vancouver. "That's where they came from in the first place," she added.[3] Within a month Vancouver city council passed a similar, if not tougher, by-law.

Central Canadian cities also responded to growing public irritation. The police chief of the Montreal Urban Community assigned a squad of 50 officers to patrol the downtown area of

Montreal on foot to ensure beggars and squeegee crews were not interfering with traffic. Violators were issued with $75 tickets for soliciting in the street. In Ottawa four downtown "business improvement" groups hired a safety patrol officer to clamp down on aggressive panhandling and other street nuisances.

In Toronto, while its task force was still working on strategies to help the homeless, city council began to consider a by-law to restrict them from begging on the streets. In particular, many motorists wanted an end to soliciting from squeegee kids. The proposal occupied Toronto's media during the early summer of 1998 before council voted it down, advised by solicitors that the city had no legal authority to regulate panhandling and might even be violating the Canadian Charter of Rights.

By the summer of 1998 when they gave this advice Toronto's solicitors would be well aware that the original Winnipeg by-law was running into trouble. The first two charges under the legislation arrived in a Winnipeg court, and the defendants who were charged failed to show up. Homeless, without addresses, there appeared to be no hope of finding them. The judge, who felt that squeegee kids always did "an admirable job" on his car windshield, threw out the charges.

The by-law was also being tested on another front. The National Anti-Poverty Organization made application to challenge the validity of the by-law under the Canadian constitution. By early fall of 1998 the city of Winnipeg was ready to consider a compromise by-law rather than go to court. In broad outline, according to a background paper prepared by the Caledon Institute of Social Policy specifically for the challenge, the settlement would involve recognition on the part of Winnipeg that individuals have a right to beg on the streets so long as they do so in a peaceful and unthreatening manner.

While the challenge to the Winnipeg by-law was a first for Canada, there had been similar challenges to anti-vagrancy by-laws in the United States. When the New York transit authority attempted to crack down on panhandlers in subway stations in the early 1990s, a federal district court judge found that panhandling was a form of free speech protected by the constitution. In his ruling the judge wrote: "While the government has an interest in preserving the quality of urban life, this interest must be discounted where the regulation has the principal effect of keeping a public problem involving human beings out of sight and therefore out of mind."[4]

In Florida a federal judge ruled in a lawsuit brought against the city of Miami by homeless people that police had no right to arrest the homeless for sleeping in public parks. A local judge in Key West also declared unconstitutional a city ordinance prohibiting the homeless from sleeping on the city's public beach. In Nevada a federal judge declared a Las Vegas anti-vagrancy law unconstitutional. A challenge against a similar city ordinance was made in Reno on behalf of a homeless man arrested for sleeping in a city park. While some challenges to local by-laws were successful in US courts, some were not.

In the end, despite a recognition of individual rights as well as enforcement problems, Canadian cities continued over the next year to consider proposals for new panhandling legislation in response to pressure from the general public and local merchants. Victoria, Surrey, Kamloops, Banff, and Halifax were all urged to consider by-laws similar to those already passed in Winnipeg, Vancouver, New Westminster, Calgary, Kelowna, Brandon, Ottawa, and Sudbury.

Even after six months Toronto's defeated by-law still had its supporters. Ontario Minister of Tourism Al Palladini, one of the supporters, wanted beggars restricted by legislation, claiming they pestered tourists and were, in general, bad for business. And, in fact, the idea had not been laid to rest. New legislation was already being drafted by the provincial government which would allow Toronto to win after all. Tabled in the Ontario Legislature in the fall of 1999, a Safe Streets Act again targeted squeegee kids and proposed stiff penalties for anyone asking their fellow citizens for money.

It would be tragic if the central issue of the homeless became the issue of recognizing or denying their right to beg or sleep in public places. In asking for help and finding a place to put their heads down, the homeless are simply trying to stay alive. More than anything, one wonders why they would even want to stay alive. The central issue is really the issue of whether the homeless are responsible for their own misfortune or whether we are all responsible. If the cause of homelessness lies in the personal deficiencies of those who are homeless, we would find among them some personally deficient Canadians who are not poor. But we would look in vain. Henry Miller, a researcher and historian of the homeless in the US, comments: "People of means, with rare and trivial exceptions, do *not* become homeless."[5]

At the root of homelessness is poverty and the shocking reality that we are now tolerating a level of poverty that leaves so many without a roof over their heads. Beyond the root cause of poverty we also tolerate a housing situation in our cities that provides little or no accommodation the poor can afford. The formula is simple—combine a growing number of poor and a growing number of expensive housing units and we have people on the streets. Add to this a failure to recognize that the mentally ill cannot manage on their own, economically or with even the simplest of life's demands, and we have even more people on the streets.

Significant social trends have contributed to this tragic evidence of two worlds in our cities, trends that have involved public policies, private-sector restructuring, and individual actions. One of these trends has been the unanticipated preference of many households since the mid-1970s to be located in the inner city, partly reversing a trend toward suburbanization that stretches back into the 19th century.

Involving the replacement of traditional multi-family housing with single-family housing, the preference for inner city residence has lowered inner city density. In the past 25 years four of Canada's major cities have suffered a combined net loss of accommodation for over 250,000 people in their central core areas. Only Vancouver with a predominance of high-rise and townhouse development for this new type of household has increased the inner city population, although within its higher density there is little housing stock at the bottom end of the market.

While Canadian suburbs have continued to provide most residential housing with seemingly unlimited space, upgrading to lower density in the inner city has reduced the amount of housing available where the poor have traditionally made their homes. These are the areas where housing used to be affordable. Few of the poor have ever been able to afford accommodation in the suburbs, let alone the cost and time spent in getting there.

The homeless are the group left behind in competition for fewer and fewer affordable housing units. Frequently unemployed and on social assistance, they have the least to spend on shelter and, given the other nagging demands on their limited incomes, like food, they are considered the most likely tenants to miss rental payments by landlords who have many others to choose from. This is the simple economics of low vacancy rates, though there are still a lingering few who believe the homeless prefer to live without permanent shelter. The problem of homelessness is explained, fundamentally, by a lack of housing the poor can afford. Most Canadians know it by now; the homeless have always known it.

Another trend contributing to homelessness in the 1980s and 1990s is the shift away from institutional care for the mentally ill. With breakthroughs in medication and with the best of intentions, the advice of medical experts in the 1960s was that psychiatric patients in mental institutions would have more successful rehabilitation on the outside. Institutions had simply become depots for dead storage. Over the next ten to 15 years they were gradually closed down.

Rescued from dead storage, the mentally ill have been moved from the protective structure of four walls into a chaotic urban environment with no walls. Whatever made us think they were capable of the simple task of taking the new miracle medication on their own? And we might further ask, what was the rush? In our unbridled enthusiasm to close down institutions, were we motivated by the desire for more effective treatment on the outside or simply by the desire to save money?

By the 1990s the answer was obvious. Money spent formerly on institutional care had not been shifted to non-institutional or community-based care. It had disappeared, leaving former or potential mental patients with as little care as they were given in the mid-19th century. Indeed our mentally ill had gone from a state of neglect to a state of neglect in just five generations.

The causes of homelessness, however, are not found only in the reversal of two long-standing trends, suburbanization and institutionalization. The best we can say about these late 20th-century reversals is that they were not intentional attempts to make life more difficult for the poor. This is not the case with public policies related to social housing. As many senior levels of government in Canada withdrew and began to download the responsibility for low-income housing to local governments in the 1980s and 1990s, no groundswell of public protest could be heard. Even municipal taxpayers who were left with the responsibility failed to protest cuts in social housing. Community groups pushed for better transit systems, traffic "calming", and even panhandling legislation, but none clamoured for low-income public housing in their neighbourhoods. In the end, social housing went through the final downloading—from municipal government to oblivion. Not many, except the poor, were sorry to see it go.

Other factors have played a role. Developers and home builders are in the business of making money, but profits from low-income housing are widely acknowledged to be low. This reality has given little incentive for new construction to serve the lowest end of the market. In addition, the poor in Canada are getting poorer, 30 percent more living below the poverty line in 1996 than in 1986 compared to total population growth of only 14 percent for the same period. In fact, Canada's 1996 poor lived a greater distance below the poverty line. Consequently a growing portion of the poor now spend more than half their incomes on rent. Even without a decline in housing supply and an increase in demand from baby boomers, low-income households with less to spend on rent than in the past are effectively denied access to the housing market.

A review of these trends that have contributed to increasing homelessness in Canada in the midst of increasing affluence may take us back further than recent history but may, in the end, answer the central question of why we are faced today with this tragic paradox.

CHAPTER 2

Abandoning the Inner City

Canada's largest cities hang like a string of Christmas tree lights across the top of North America. Most are no further north than 50 degrees latitude, a reflection of the rigor of Canadian winters and the pattern of early railway lines laid out across often unfriendly terrain.

Each city has its own uniqueness, reflecting its place in Canadian history and its capacity to adapt as the national economy moved from fur trade to farming to industry over 300 years. Quebec City keeps its old world atmosphere, Edmonton its forward-looking frontier character, Toronto its facade of self-confidence. Though individually unique, however, cities in Canada have much in common with each other and with cities throughout the world.

Historians and geographers have documented these similarities in extensive studies of worldwide urbanization. They have traced rural-urban shifts of population which have brought us to today's high proportion of urban dwellers (almost 80 percent in North America, northwestern Europe, Australia, and New Zealand) and they have traced shifts of populations *within* cities. Though its urban development has lagged, Canada has not strayed far from the general pattern.

The shift of world populations from rural to urban areas has been described as a major transformation of society. Urban historians would generally agree that the significant growth of large cities began in the 19th century accompanied by, and caused by, industrialization. In Europe first, especially Great Britain, and later in the United States massive migrations of people from rural farmland to urban centres spelled the beginning of an urban way of life for most of the world's population.

In Canada the process was only in its infancy by mid-century with populations of 57,000 and 30,000 respectively for Montreal and Toronto.[1] Over the next 40 years, however, the populations of those two cities more than quadrupled, growing to 254,000 and 180,000. In the western provinces, although towns were beginning to spring up along new railway lines, it would be another 20 years before any grew to a significant size. Winnipeg's population reached 135,000 in 1911 and Vancouver's over 100,000. Yet despite the slower urbanization of the West, 50 percent of Canada's total population lived in cities by 1921.

The process of rural-urban migration has been seemingly irreversible. Of greater relevance to the issue of homelessness, however, is the migration of populations within cities. In one form or another, substantial internal migration generally became a characteristic of cities as their populations grew in size and density. As a result many cities in a relatively new country like Canada, where agricultural and rural life predominated, had not grown enough to send residents in search of more space until the turn of the century. Older and larger urban centres, both in Canada and the rest of the world, began the process earlier. The dates are not as important as the direction of the shift from the inner city to the outskirts—the whole phenomenon of suburbanization—which has had a profound impact on the nature of urban growth and the lifestyles of urban residents.

The development of suburbs was perhaps inevitable. The central areas of newly industrialized cities were soon characterized by congestion and questionable air. By the middle to late 19th century many affluent residents were leaving the central core of large American cities and the Canadian cities of Toronto and Montreal. They sought not only the cleaner air and lower density of the suburbs but a separation from the poor who had little choice but to reside within walking distance of the inner city factories where they worked.

An early US example was the allure of Beacon Hill to Boston's upper class when a Boston resident purchased and developed land for housing a distance from the city centre in a pattern that would be repeated hundreds of times over the next century. In New York by mid-century the affluent had moved to newly developed Gramercy Park. In San Francisco what was to become Nob Hill was attracting many city residents who could afford to leave downtown congestion behind.

A study of Montreal in roughly the same period has been done by Canadian urban historian David Hanna. He describes how landowners on the south slope of Mount Royal subdivided the lower portion of their estates (from the present Sherbrooke Street south) and attracted residents from the older central district into more pleasant surroundings. In Toronto, still not rivalling Montreal in size at mid-century, middle- and upper-class residents were already starting to settle in suburbs north of the city limits at Bloor Street (in the Village of Yorkville and in Rosedale) and in Parkdale to the west of the city limits. In these early population moves, suburbanites used their own transportation to commute back and forth to the city centre.

Commuting was made easier by 1860 with the development of new transportation technology. Street railways (with horse-drawn streetcars) appeared in New York, Baltimore, Philadelphia, Pittsburgh, Chicago, Cincinnati, Boston, Montreal, Toronto, and Halifax, carrying passengers from the core of the city to the periphery and making suburban living a choice for an even greater portion of the city's well-to-do. In Toronto a new horse-drawn street railway began operation on Yonge, King and Queen streets. On September 10, 1861, the *Toronto Globe* reported in detail on the inaugural opening. When the first streetcar was ready to be pulled along the newly laid tracks, according to the *Globe*, "a grand cheer arose from the assembled multitude." Civic dignitaries proudly took their seats in the modern-looking conveyance and, perhaps unwisely in retrospect, an artillery band "playing spirited airs" took up its position on the car roof. Heading toward Bloor Street amid cheers, the car ran off the tracks no more than a few hundred feet from its starting point. This potential public relations disaster failed to dampen the spirit of the occasion, however. Dignitaries and band members disembarked, hoisted the car back in place, and resumed their seats as the driver and the horses tried again to see if they could get it right.

In Halifax five years later a new street railway was launched with similar fanfare. As the moment arrived, a marching band of the 4th Regiment led a procession of five brand new horse-cars filled with the Lieutenant-Governor and other dignitaries and managed to set them on their way without mishap. When fully operating, the Halifax street railway service ran from downtown Inglis Street to a depot in suburban Richmond, near the foot of present-day Duffus Street. Housing and industrial development took place rapidly at the Richmond end of the line, becoming Halifax's North End before the turn of the century.

In Montreal a horse-drawn street railway was also established in the 1860s. Ten years later when the line was extended west along Ste-Catherines Street to what was to become Westmount, the area at the end of the line was open farmland. A steady stream of upper-class Montreal residents began to buy up lots close to the terminus, starting Westmount on its way to becoming one of the most popular suburbs for Montreal commuters.

By the turn of the century most horse-drawn streetcars had been replaced with electric streetcars, some reaching a speed as great as 14 miles an hour. Electric railways were a major impetus to suburban development. In the decade before World War I Toronto's street railway stretched from the foot of Yonge Street north to St. Clair and from downtown Yonge west to High Park and east to Victoria Park. In Halifax horse-drawn streetcars were replaced with electric cars along the 20-year-old Barrington Street route and new tracks were laid as far as Willow Park, the developing West End in need of a public transportation link with the city.

In Vancouver an electric street railway system was in place by 1890, and 16 track miles were installed by the turn of the century. Vancouver suburbs developed along streetcar lines in a manner similar to that of other North American cities in the same period. To the west the car line opened up land subdivision in Kitsilano and later in West Point Grey; to the east Grandview began to fill. To the south the Shaughnessy Heights subdivision was developed. Vancouver residents who could afford spacious Shaughnessy Heights lots left the density of the inner city and moved to the tree-lined streets of the new subdivision. Served by a street railway line, Shaughnessy

Heights began to be settled in the five years before World War I, a considerable time before the automobile was in popular use.

The Ottawa Electric Street Railway opened in 1900, contributing to the creation of new suburbs in Ottawa over the next 15 years. By 1913 streetcars were carrying 25 million passengers a year. Subdivisions in the Glebe and Ottawa South were developed south along Bank Street, attracting from the central area home buyers who could commute by streetcar to work downtown. To the west development pushed past the city limits at Churchill Street into rural Nepean Township and surrounded the village of Westboro with its population of only 900 in 1910. Development tied in with streetcar service running from Westboro to Ottawa every 20 minutes initially and every five minutes within a year or two. Advertisements of real estate agents for the Highland Park and McKellar Townsite areas described acres of rolling land dotted with trees "only a few minutes walk from the street railway station."[2]

Calgary, with a population of only 45,000 by 1911, also showed signs of suburban development over the next five years. Calgary residents began to build and move into homes north and south of the business centre, the location of new residential areas reflecting the location of streetcar routes. Over 50 streetcars ran along almost 60 miles of track. North of the Bow River new tracks facilitated the development of Parkdale and Westmount. To the southwest negotiations for street railway extensions took place between developers and the city, resulting in the new residential areas of Tuxedo Park and Elbow Park. The subdivision of Mount Royal was also settled as upper-class families looked for more spacious lots and more attractive surroundings than the inner part of the city could provide.

Montreal, after using horse-drawn streetcars for 30 years, switched to an electric railway system in 1892. When the line reached Côte Ste-Catherine the old gardens and orchards of Outremont were subdivided and transformed into city suburbs. On the other slope of the mountain, Westmount's growth continued at an even greater pace than earlier and, by the turn of the century, land in Westmount was high-priced.

Winnipeg's street railway was carrying over three million passengers a year by 1900. Early residential settlement in Winnipeg had been generally in the areas around Main Street and the Red River, later spreading west (but still north of the Assiniboine) and east across the Red into the small settlement of St. Boniface. New bridges and new car lines, however, were an incentive to suburban development around the turn of the century. The street railway crossed the new Main Street bridge over the Red River allowing the rapid expansion of St. Boniface and later ran south of St. Boniface into the suburb of St. Vital. Tracks also ran north along Main and made a major contribution to the suburban development of Kildonan. The Osborne and Maryland bridges across the Assiniboine carried street car riders to their new homes in the suburb of Fort Rouge.

In these early suburbs of Canadian cities land developers targeted upper-class home buyers. At the end of World War I, however, new transportation technology made it possible for the expanding urban middle class to join the exodus to areas at the edge of the city. The automobile, especially as it reached the stage of mass production in the US, changed the face of North American cities dramatically. From a toy of the rich before 1900 the automobile became a must-have possession of over eight million Americans and almost half-a-million Canadians by 1920. The automobile, unlike the street railway, allowed urban residents to go *where* they wanted *when* they wanted, choosing their own route and taking the whole family for the cost of a single ride. With this kind of flexibility and with the economic reality that land prices decreased with each mile from the centre of the city, the automobile made low-density suburban living more feasible for many who were anxious to escape the inner city.

Even before the North American middle class began its 90-year love affair with the automobile, it had already shown its preference for home ownership over renting. As early as 1920 more than 58 percent of Canadian households owned their homes and throughout the next 70 years the percentage increased steadily.[3] (In the 1990s almost 73 percent of Canadians owned their homes. This increase reflected two related trends—home ownership increased steadily from the inner city to the fringe, and the fringe became home to more people than the inner city.)

The growing popularity of the automobile and the ideal of an individual family home resulted in a suburban boom in the 1920s.

On the outskirts of many major US cities suburbs sprang up, among them Coral Gables in Florida, and Elmwood Park near Chicago. In Canada the pattern was being repeated. Housing development in Winnipeg increased rapidly south of the Assiniboine River as residential real estate near busy, downtown Portage Avenue became less attractive. House lots in River Heights promised less density and, though just beyond walking distance from most places of work in downtown Winnipeg, they were easily reached by automobile.

Similarly in Hamilton, middle-class families began to move into the new suburb of Westdale to the west of the city where household heads could commute back and forth to work by car while their children were raised in healthy suburban air. Other examples were Forest Hill Village in Toronto, the Uplands in Victoria, and the further settlement of Vancouver suburbs started in the pre-war period— Shaughnessy Heights, Dunbar, and West Point Grey. Streetcar service also continued to all these areas, but the middle class had by then discovered the joy of driving.

The story of the 1920s development of Kingsway Park, a subdivision on the western fringe of Toronto, is told by urban historian Ross Patterson and provides an example of some of the ways and means of suburban development during that period. Land developer Robert Home Smith had assembled 3,000 acres of prime land in the Humber Valley between 1906 and 1912, long before the widespread use of the automobile. In the 1920s housing construction began on subdivided lots of his land assembly which he named Kingsway Park.

Typical of suburban development of the period, construction was not undertaken by the developer but by individual builders, each undertaking only two or three houses. Nor did the developer provide waterlines, sewers, or street lighting. These were the responsibility of the municipality (Etobicoke Township, in the case of Kingsway Park) in the expectation that the cost of such services would be recouped later through increased property taxes. The developer controlled the value and quality of housing in the new suburb by approving all house plans and by targeting middle-class families in his marketing.

By 1930 Kingsway Park had been successful in attracting this particular client group. Middle-class families were also the target of developers in River Heights, Westdale, and Uplands, among others. For Montreal residents, the new Town of Mount Royal had the same appeal. The Town of Mount Royal, however, had its own unique selling point for commuters—a new tunnel and railway line pushed through the mountain from downtown, an engineering feat of the Canadian Northern Railway.

The Depression of the 1930s brought a decline in suburban housing development, though automobile registrations levelled off in only two years of that decade. Residential construction was further held back during World War II. But activity in the post-war period can only be described as a construction boom. Suburban expansion surpassed that of all earlier periods and was no longer confined to the upper and middle classes. The automobile was now within the financial reach of the working class. Just as anxious as higher-income families to enjoy the lower density of the suburbs, working-class families could finally make it work economically. The increased strength of labour unions gained during the war years, combined with the lifting of wartime wage ceilings, had raised the average worker's income substantially. Car and home ownership became dreams that could be realized.

Access to home ownership was also made easier with the creation in 1945 of the Central Mortgage and Housing Corporation (CMHC) which acted as a mortgage lender itself or guaranteed mortage loans made by other lenders such as trust companies. Since one of the objectives of the new CMHC was to support the provision of adequate housing to Canadians (and especially to returning war veterans), interest rates on mortgages were set lower than market rates, down payments were lowered, and amortization periods were increased.

It was the automobile, however, that made it all possible. In the post-war years earlier suburbs clustering around streetcar lines were expanded and whole new subdivisions appeared in areas that were previously out of reach. In Vancouver, for example, both types of new development took place. To the northeast older suburbs expanded until they spilled over into northern Burnaby. The automobile now allowed commuters living in the northeast area to settle beyond the end of the streetcar line and indeed it soon became the most frequently used mode of transportation.

To the south large farms in Richmond were subdivided and middle-class families were attracted into new suburbs. The later post-war period brought even greater expansion to Richmond with the completion of the Oak Street Bridge in 1957, creating access by automobile to the developing suburban area in the south. In fact, the need for bridges and other crossings of inlets and river tributaries in the Vancouver area presented a major challenge to settlement to the south in the post-war years. The new Deas Island Tunnel completed two years after the Oak Street Bridge was a further attempt to meet this need. It allowed commuters to settle in new subdivisions in Ladner and further south in upscale Tsawwassen Over the next decade Coquitlam, Port Coquitlam, and Port Moody were Vancouver suburbs experiencing rapid growth. The lack of public transportation from these areas into Vancouver made commuters dependent entirely on the automobile for many years.

On the east coast in Halifax the needs of returning veterans also had to be met. Housing development soon covered the last open spaces in the West End with new suburbs. The temporary barracks of Camp Chebucto were torn down to make room for the Westmount housing development; houses also went up in the Armcrest subdivision and on new streets alongside the Dutch Village Road. The automobile also made it feasible for Halifax residents to commute from areas near the St. Margaret's Bay Road or further south from the village of Spryfield growing rapidly in the post-war period.

In post-war Ottawa the city's western limits were extended as Ottawa annexed a portion of Nepean Township to accommodate the demand for housing. Farms in the Britannia area in former Nepean were bought up and subdivided, at first by small contractors purchasing enough acreage to create as few as 20 lots, but later by large developers. The older neighbourhoods like Lorna Park were filled in with new housing, and new neighbourhoods were developed—Queensway Park by the late 1950s and later Lincoln Heights. The automobile made it feasible for home buyers to consider living in these previously remote areas on the western fringe. In fact, by the late 1950s the last of the streetcars were taken out of service to the west end.

To the south and to the east of the Rideau River suburban Alta

Vista also came into being to accommodate some of the immediate post-war housing needs of Ottawa. Commuters could be at work in Centretown in 15 to 20 minutes by car. To the southwest the area of Nepean Township that had escaped the annexation of 1950 became one large Ottawa suburb over the next 15 years. Large developments were increasingly the trend, creating the extensive Bayshore area, a Nepean suburb near the Ottawa boundary line, and the even larger community of Kanata in March Township to the far west. Kanata, especially, was accessible only by car.

In Toronto immediately following the war the housing shortage was especially acute. New construction was stimulated by this unprecedented demand (estimated to be at least 50,000 housing units for Toronto alone) and by low-interest mortgages under the new National Housing Act (NHA). As in other Canadian cities, early post-war suburbs in Toronto offered little diversity. In the interest of economy builders tended to repeat the same housing design over and over along streets laid out in an orderly grid. More than one homeowner commuting from work to his home in a new "NHA" subdivision turned on to the wrong driveway by mistake. This type of housing sprang up in subdivisions north of Lawrence Avenue in North York Township and later in subdivisions north of Wilson Avenue. An exception to this uniformity in the early construction period was Thorncrest Village in Etobicoke, a community made up of roughly 170 houses on wide lots along meandering streets.

After 1950 the development of Don Mills to the north and east of Toronto was a forerunner of large-scale developments across Canada in which one developer planned, subdivided, and serviced the community while controlling the quality of houses put up by individual builders. Schools, shopping centres, and green space were part of the community plan. In total, over 8,000 housing units were created in Don Mills. Toronto suburbs continued to expand north of Sheppard, then north of Finch, then north of Steeles avenues. Rural concession roads became six-lane thoroughfares for automobiles, of which every suburban household had at least one. To the east Scarborough and to the west Etobicoke were areas of new housing.

Similarly by the early 1950s Calgary broke away from the old grid subdivisions of the first wave of post-war housing and, in fact, of housing in pre-war periods. Experiencing rapid growth over the 15 years following the war, Calgary's population increase was not only the result of the resettlement of war veterans. It was also caused by heavy migration into the city from rural areas and other urban areas in the West. To accommodate this growth the city expanded outward in all directions except where limited by the industrial and wholesale district to the east. Fairview, Wildwood, and Glendale were examples of Calgary subdivisions accessible for the most part by car.

Winnipeg also watched automobile suburbs grow dramatically at the end of World War II. Wildwood Park in Fort Garry was one of the earliest subdivisions. Surrounded on three sides by the Red River, it pushed the city's built-up area southward. On the other side of the Red a more extensive development, Lyndale Drive, went up in Norwood. The old Riverview area which is today encircled by Churchill Drive was another area of rapid expansion in the post-war period. The population also spread west along Portage into St. James. The Riverbend Crescent cul-de-sac overlooking the Assiniboine River was an early post-war development and the larger Silver Heights subdivision on the other side of Portage was built up a few years later.

In Montreal in the post-war period housing went up in the Town of Mount Royal, Hampstead, Côte-Saint-Luc, Anjou, Rosemont, St-Michel, and Mercier. All except the Town of Mount Royal housed new suburbanites who commuted to work by car.

During the three decades following the end of World War II suburban growth far outpaced the growth of the entire metropolitan area in major Canadian cities. The growth of new suburbs during the period ranged from 250 percent to over 800 percent. In 1948 only 32 percent of the population in what would later become Metro lived outside the boundaries of the City of Toronto. By 1966 the Metro population outside city boundaries accounted for 63 percent. In greater Vancouver the suburban population in the 1950s represented only 41 percent of the total; 20 years later the suburban share had risen to 61 percent.

In Winnipeg during the same period the municipalities surrounding the City of Winnipeg grew far more quickly (an increase of 140 percent) than did the city itself (an increase of only four percent), dramatically increasing the suburban population in sheer numbers but also increasing its share of the total population of greater Winnipeg from a third to well over a half. Montreal's greater metropolitan area also became more suburban as population growth mushroomed on the outskirts (by 196 percent) and slowed down within city limits (an increase of only 19 percent).

Urban ecologists contend that spatial considerations are a major influence in city growth and that over time cities grow outward in concentric circles or in corridors moving outward radially, following rivers or transportation routes. Demographers, too, are interested in the way urban residents move outward, but they attribute migration of any kind to what they call *push* and *pull* factors. For example, the *push* factors of migration within cities would be congestion and poor air which push populations from the city core, while *pull* factors would be the low density and clean air of the open land at the fringe of the city. In any particular population move, according to demographers, migrants may be more pushed than pulled, and vice versa.

Economists would argue that, since the availability of land increases as one moves away from the centre of the city, the price of land at the outskirts will be lower. Other things being equal, lower prices will increase demand and there will be an exodus from the city to the suburbs. When other things are not equal, like the relative cost of getting to work or the time it takes, home buyers will pass up the low prices.

There is another element, as some surveys have shown, which is not quite captured in any of these theories. People often move to the suburbs because they want the best possible environment for their children—safer, healthier, more likely to have schools that attract the best teachers, and, most important, suitable social contacts. In other words, a move away from the inner city is an upward move and, put in its best light, it's done for the children.

While all these arguments can be made about the urban population immediately following World War II, the boom of suburban expansion is best explained by two developments specific only to that period—a shortage of housing due to a drastic decline in construction during the Depression decade (and throughout the war years) and a sudden increase in demand as servicemen returned and established families.

In the early post-war years the disadvantages of a home in the inner city—congestion and proximity to industry—were not as great a factor for the home buyer as finding a home *anywhere*. In other words, economic laws of supply and demand played a larger role than the push-pull laws of migration. "Anywhere" turned out to be where developers (with considerable support from the federal government) were soon ready with a supply of housing—on the outer fringes of the city where undeveloped land was still available and cheap. Early post-war subdivisions had little in the way of amenities—row upon row of box-like houses, some developers offering as many as three house styles among 1,500 houses in a subdivision. Demand was high; and the speed of meeting it was more important than what might be considered frills. And certainly the frills were not expected.

When the last of the baby boomers were born around the mid-1950s, however, their parents were presented with more housing options than in the immediate post-war period. Subdivision planning had become a little more inspired, housing styles a little more numerous. Home buyers with middle-class aspirations could afford to think of upward mobility as much as the number of bedrooms in choosing a home. One of the options was a home in the earlier suburbs filled up originally in the 1920s and now inside the ever-expanding city limits. In the 1950s, however, the new, not the old, was valued. Wide lots and ranch-style bungalows were the home buyer's dream; few took up the option of 30-year-old houses in old suburbs. Moreover, houses of the 1920s suburbs were only beginning to turn over. Although driveways were no longer used by toddlers riding tricycles, they still had a use for teenagers borrowing the family car. The nests would not be empty for another five to ten years.

As a result, like the generation before, parents of the late baby boomers chose the suburbs for the benefits they offered to their growing children—good schools, safe environment, and suitable contacts. They settled down and raised their baby boomers who would one day decide that the *old* not the new was valuable, that 45 minutes a day in an automobile was not how they wanted to spend their time, and that the responsibilities of parenthood could wait until dual careers were established.

CHAPTER 3

Reclaiming the Inner City

Inevitably as a rapidly growing portion of the urban population began to take up residence in the suburbs, the inner city was left to the poor. Former single-family homes of the middle class became boarding homes or rooming houses as quickly as investors could transform them. As a result, density increased in the old residential areas. As many as 20 people could be accommodated in some of the more substantial single-family homes.

Many of these same neighbourhoods fell victim to street widening in a new era of throughways. They had lost their middle-class voice at city hall. Neighbourhoods were sliced up by traffic corridors, but for the new boarding house residents a sense of neighbourhood was not yet important. It would be another ten or 15 years before the most articulate and militant among them would join forces to stop the expressways. For the most part, however, they were boarders and tenants with little political cohesion or influence.

During that ten or 15 years the former tree-lined streets began to lose their trees, former middle-class schools began to lose good qualified staff or closed altogether, and local merchants began to cater to singles rather than families. Absentee landlords provided the minimum of maintenance, letting good housing stock deteriorate and lowering property values.

Alongside these developments in the old middle-class residential areas of the inner city, the traditional slums nearby were undergoing change. These slum areas adjacent to the central business district (and the diminishing number of factories) were made up of a mixture of small homeowners and tenants in old deteriorating housing. A few homeowners had created a sense of permanence over the years with modest gardens and valiant upkeep of wood-frame houses built too long ago. But landlords hung on to most of the housing stock, waiting for expansion of the downtown commercial area when they might realize a good return on their investments. In the meantime, they charged rents the poor could just afford if they bought fewer groceries.

Rent demands and substandard living conditions were a constant reminder to tenants of their place in the economic order and they vied with landlords to see who could contribute the most to letting the premises fall into disrepair. Despite these not-so-hidden hostilities, tenants and small homeowners alike felt an attachment to their neighbourhood. To the larger urban community, however, the slums were simply blight.

In the late 1940s the federal government unveiled plans for the old slums. Cities could demolish their eyesores with federal and provincial help. The National Housing Act, with the dual goals of providing adequate housing for Canadians and creating employment for the influx of returning servicemen, had come into effect a few years earlier. As we have seen, the Act provided for more accessible mortgages, most of which covered new suburban homes for veterans and their families. Stimulation of the construction industry was more than successful in the suburbs. Now a new program of slum clearance in the city core, so-called urban renewal, would also create employment. Under NHA terms the demolition of slums and the construction of low-rent public housing in their place could be undertaken in Canadian cities. The federal government would fund half the cost of slum clearance and 75 percent of the cost of public housing.

Municipalities were slow in taking up the federal offer of slum clearance. By the mid-1950s only Toronto had applied. Forty-two acres of "blighted land" were cleared in Toronto's Regent Park and construction started on a proposed 1,056 low-rent housing units. Despite a slow start, however, eight other urban renewal applications were approved during the remainder of the 1950s.[1] Projects were launched in St. John's, Newfoundland, in Les Habitations Jeanne Mance in Montreal, in the Jacob Street project in downtown Halifax, in Moss Park in Toronto, in a 15-acre area near Windsor's City Hall, in the eastern part of Saint John, in Sarnia's Bluewater area, and in Strathcona in Vancouver. By 1960 over 400 acres of slums had been cleared.

Over the next eight years Canadian cities took part in the federal urban renewal program with even greater enthusiasm. In the next four years alone another 450 acres were cleared. New projects were undertaken in Winnipeg, Hamilton, Ottawa, Kingston, Regina, Victoria, Burlington, Calgary, Trois-Rivières, Amherst, Dartmouth, Sault Ste. Marie, Sudbury, Medicine Hat, North Battleford, and Port Arthur, among others. Four cities with projects already underway also applied to clear new slum areas.

Suddenly in 1969 the government suspended approval of all new projects pending the findings of a federal task force set up to look into the program's effectiveness. Throughout the 20-year existence of the urban renewal program over 13,000 housing units were demolished and over 20,000 residents displaced.

The unintended consequences of urban renewal in Canada (and the US) are now well-known. That they were not anticipated at the time is due to the priority given to removing blight and creating employment. After 20 years the federal Minister of Housing, Robert Andras, announced that as a result of urban renewal there had been a net loss in low-income housing stock in Canada. Among other findings, the task force appointed by the ministry found that the promised alternative housing for displaced residents was frequently unsatisfactory. In addition, the task force claimed, "communities are dispersed and long-standing and vital social links shattered."[2] In most cases, having been relocated to temporary quarters for two or more years during construction, former slum residents did not return to their old neighbourhoods even though they had been faced with higher housing costs after they had been forced to move. Many stated that one displacement had been sufficiently disrupting—and the old neighbourhood attachment was certainly missing in the new alien government housing project.

Although it was too late for the old slum areas, new policies of the federal government spared the rooming house areas, not far away, from permanent destruction by the bulldozer. Government-sponsored demolition was finished, a policy that saved the life of much of Canada's old housing stock in the inner city. An emphasis on rehabilitation and renovation in the 1970s took the place of large-scale demolition with the introduction of new federal assistance under the Neighbourhood Improvement Program (NIP) and the Residential Rehabilitation Assistance Program (RRAP).

In some cities, especially in the prairies, these financial incentives helped central neighbourhoods to avoid further decline. In Winnipeg NIP and RRAP were followed by the Winnipeg Core Area Initiative in the 1980s which was intended to revitalize the inner city rather than simply to halt decline. Funded in equal shares by federal, provincial, and municipal governments, the project provided funding for new housing units as well as renovations and repairs (among many other core area development activities). The new units replaced some, but certainly not all, of the units lost during the previous 15-year period. Renovation funding for existing units allowed improvements to more than 10 percent of the inner city housing stock. But in these cities—either holding their own against further decline or trying to turn things around—most new housing was created with government assistance or incentives. With suburban locations still preferred by homeowners, there was relatively little private reinvestment in central residential areas. Inner city housing remained predominantly low-income housing.

In Canada's largest cities, however, and even in Halifax with a population of only 220,000 in 1971, other trends began to overshadow government activity. The shift in emphasis to rehabilitation and renovation took the form of private investment in core neighbourhoods. Among several reasons for this renewed interest on the part of private homeowners in the central areas of Canadian cities and of cities of the US and Europe, new occupational developments and new lifestyles were making suburban living less attractive. The middle class began to reclaim the inner city, not only rescuing it from decline but dramatically upgrading its housing with serious consequences for the poor.

The way the urban population tended to arrange itself in urban space had developed a predictable pattern in the first three-quarters of the 20th century. Upper- and middle-class homeowners moved away from the city centre, leaving behind housing stock that decreased in value until it came within the budgets of the poor. So predictable was the pattern that urban specialists were comfortable that one or two internal migration laws described the major trends and all other developments could be explained in reference to those well-tested laws. Beginning in the 1970s, however, the old urban laws of movement from the core to the periphery of the city were not accurately describing new patterns of settlement. Middle-class households had begun to appear in significant numbers in the inner city.

The intruders (as they were called by Hugh Garner in a 1976 novel[3]) were buying old deteriorating houses of the poor and converting, often restoring, them into fashionable middle-class homes. Another group of intruders moved into high-rise condominiums. Almost unnoticed at first, their numbers increased and gradually changed the socio-economic status of the central area of many Canadian cities. In the early years of this new development, upgrading of old houses was called whitepainting; later it became more commonly known as gentrification. Condominium apartment construction, although not actually a physical upgrading of old housing stock, was nonetheless part of the entire process of inner city revitalization and clearly contributed to the upgrading of the inner city's socio-economic status.

There are several theories in explanation of this reverse pattern of migration. Perhaps the most widely accepted is that inner city revitalization is yet another outcome of the shift to a post-industrial economy in Canada and other developed countries over the past quarter-century. Almost by definition, post-industrialism has involved an increase in managerial, professional, and other white-collar occupations as blue-collar occupations have declined. Urban residents in white-collar occupations generally work in downtown offices. Since the deteriorating housing areas and the growing number of office buildings are side by side in the inner city, there seems to be a perfect fit. After all, didn't the factory workers of the past live in the inner city to be near their work?

Unfortunately post-industrialism as a theory to explain gentrification doesn't go far enough. Factory workers stayed in the inner city because they had to; they lacked the financial resources to commute daily to and from the suburbs. In contrast, the new professional/managerial class is anything but short of financial resources. If these new workers choose to make their homes in the suburbs, they can afford to get there by car, go-train, or express bus. Moreover, the factory whistle doesn't blow for them at eight o'clock. The question remains, given that a post-industrial society has a larger proportion of office workers, why have they turned their backs on the suburbs?

There are also explanations of inner city revitalization that are reluctant to give up the old laws of outward migration. The fact that there has been a middle-class interest in upgrading deteriorating housing is explained by the housing market—suburban housing, the argument goes, has become overpriced, and buyers have been forced to look at cheaper alternatives, a temporary phenomenon that will correct itself when suburban prices return to normal. While the housing market theory is attractive in its economic purity and logic, the market has failed to correct itself over the past 20 years, leaving the theory unproven. In the meantime, many homeowners have still bought in the suburbs despite overpricing. There is little reason to believe gentrifiers are living in the inner city because they have more patience than others waiting for market corrections.

Another explanation for inner city changes has been demographic developments, such as smaller households and delayed family formation, which have rendered the family orientation of the suburbs irrelevant. And still another explanation has been the disenchantment with commuting as the suburbs have sprawled further and further and automobile traffic has grown heavier and heavier.

As the trend toward gentrification became more persistent in the late 1970s urban geographers and planners began to undertake statistical research and other studies, none more comprehensive than the study completed by David Ley for Canada Mortgage and Housing in 1985. Ley's study resulted in several significant findings and put an end to much of the guesswork in attempting to explain the change in inner city areas. Because of the light shed by his study of major Canadian cities, it may be useful to look at his findings in some detail. Using measures of educational level and occupation, Ley found marked increases in socio-economic status from 1971 to

1981 in the central areas of most of Canada's major cities.

Having identified that major cities were experiencing inner city revitalization, Ley's study went on to search for explanations. As expected, the most significant finding was that the reappearance of upper- and middle-class residents in core areas was strongly associated with the growth of offices and a downtown workforce. This growth, an indicator of the shift to a service or white-collar economy characteristic of a post-industrial society, was most marked in cities with higher degrees of gentrification.

The second significant finding in Ley's study was more surprising than the white-collar finding. The study found that gentrification was associated with the preference of new inner city buyers or tenants for a certain lifestyle or set of values. In other words, the amenities offered in the inner city—entertainment and cultural facilities, parks and recreation, and in some cases a natural environmental amenity such as a waterfront or mountain view—made a better fit with the pro-urban lifestyle of gentrifiers than did the blandness of the suburbs.

Statistical research into reasons for inner city revitalization also showed that a tight housing market played a modest but not very significant role. Where rental vacancies were low, house prices high, and new housing starts declining throughout the entire metropolitan area, the trend toward gentrification in the central core was somewhat stronger. Indeed the argument that high prices in the suburbs forced homeowners into the inner city when they would prefer to be elsewhere was not as strongly supported as the argument that a new middle class of white-collar workers chose the inner city mainly because of its lifestyle appeal. Similarly, demographic explanations that relate specifically to "baby boom" homeowners were not shown to be strong in Ley's research. Inner city revitalization did not appear to be solely the result of a disproportion of city residents in the 20- to 35-year age group, female participation in the labour force, or smaller households (either single persons or couples who had delayed family formation).

With an emphasis on quality of life rather than the housing market or demographic demands, a new population has gradually emerged in Canada's inner cities over the past 25 years. The restoration and renovation of old houses and the construction of new condominiums has generally taken place in an area near pleasant natural surroundings or on the fringes of upscale residential areas, and sometimes with the advantages of both. A look at the changes in five Canadian cities reveals a pattern of inner city revitalization common to major cities in North America. In Canada the pattern is most advanced in Ottawa, Halifax, Toronto, Montreal, and Vancouver.

In Ottawa there has been significant upgrading in the central areas near the picturesque Rideau Canal. In Centre Town to the west of the canal, much of the housing has been affected by redevelopment since the early 1970s. Renovated single-family homes built in the late 19th century, many of them converted to rooming and boarding houses in the period following World War II, share the same street with new three-storey townhouse construction. On renovated housing old brickwork and trim have been rejuvenated and many exteriors have been faithfully restored to their original appearance. South of Centre Town the Glebe is now home to another group of gentrifiers attracted by the architectural quality of older houses. On the streets from First Avenue to the canal on the south, extensive upgrading of single-family homes has taken place over the past 20 years. Renovation has included both row housing and detached houses. The transformation of the eastern section of this group of streets is all but complete. It is now predominantly a middle-class neighbourhood.

On the other side of the canal Sandy Hill, a residential area of houses over 100 years old, has been considerably upgraded. Although redevelopment has taken place unevenly, many detached, semi-detached and row houses have new exteriors. Northeast of Sandy Hill at the junction of the Ottawa and Rideau rivers, New Edinburgh, one of the oldest areas of Ottawa, was also one of the first to be gentrified. Restored 19th-century single-family homes and newly-built 20th-century townhouses stand alongside each other on Mackay, Crichton, Keefer, and other streets. To the west of downtown more recent changes have been seen on streets west of Kent. A mixture of new townhouses and old detached houses, now restored, is a common sight on James, Lisgar, and other Ottawa streets that date back to the 1880s.

The revitalization of Ottawa's inner city has been going on for over two decades. Within the walls of the renovated houses, new townhouse condominiums, and upmarket high-rises, residents themselves have taken on a new look. Over 25 years the proportion of inner city residents with university completion has increased dramatically.[4] In the gentrified Centre Town area alone the proportion of residents with university degrees reached 59 percent compared to 30 percent in the whole metropolitan area.

There has also been significant change in the types of jobs held by inner city residents. While the majority were blue-collar workers in the 1960s, managerial, professional, service, and other white-collar jobs predominated in the 1990s. Ninety-eight percent of jobs held by Centre Town residents were in white-collar occupations by 1996, a higher proportion than in the metropolitan area as a whole.

One gentrified area bound on the east and south by the canal in Ottawa's Glebe district gives a simple before-and-after picture. Residents with university degrees in that area rose from 10 percent of the population to almost 60 percent over 25 years. White-collar occupations grew from less than half of all occupations to 95 percent. Educational and occupational changes also brought changes in income. In 1971 the average household income in this area of the Glebe was 14 percent *lower* than the average for the city as a whole; in 1996 it was 18 percent *higher.*

The density of Ottawa's inner city lowered significantly during the 25-year period. Almost 20,000 fewer people were housed within the same geographical boundaries as the number of rooming houses declined sharply and single-family units took their place. New construction of condominium high-rises in the central district and single-family housing in Le Breton failed to stop the trend. And this population decrease took place while the population of the entire metropolitan area increased by over 400,000.

Children who had appeared to be non-existent in the new gentrified areas of the 1970s and early 1980s were more evident in the 1990s. Of the shrinking population of the inner city of Ottawa they still represented 13 percent, suggesting that earlier childless gentrifiers had simply delayed family formation. There was little evidence they left the central areas once families were started.

The revitalization of Halifax's central area originally received its impetus in the late 1960s when some of its valued historic properties along the harbour were threatened with demolition. Following the public outcry and the withdrawal of wrecking crews, the city adopted a policy of historical preservation, but for many old homes and buildings it was too late. There had already been extensive demolition as part of urban renewal in the downtown area.

With this rekindled interest in Halifax history, upgrading of old housing stock began near Citadel Hill and spread into the old south suburbs from Spring Garden Road south to Inglis Street. Gentrifiers have restored the old wooden houses and cottages typical of early to mid-19th century Halifax, saving the popular Scottish dormers and the flat-front facades of the period. To the west houses have been upgraded in the area near Dalhousie University. Just north of the downtown area new homeowners have also restored Victorian detached and terraced housing (as well as older cottages) along Falkland, Bauer, and other streets near the Halifax Commons. While these older neighbourhoods were the earliest to be gentrified, residents have also started to restore housing in the Hydrostone neighbourhood to the north, an area rebuilt after the Halifax explosion of 1917.

Two decades of change in Halifax's inner city have lowered its density to an even greater extent than in Ottawa. While Ottawa housed almost 20,000 fewer people in the inner city by 1996, Halifax with only a third of Ottawa's population lost the same number. The inner city population decreased by a quarter during the same period that the entire Halifax population increased by almost a half.

There were changes in socio-economic status as well. The proportion of Halifax inner city residents with university completion rose sharply—in some areas the proportion reached over half in contrast to a quarter of the population with university degrees in the city as a whole.

The educationally upgraded inner city also changed its occupational profile. Managerial, professional, and other white-collar occupations followed a similar pattern as the growth in Ottawa. In one area adjacent to downtown Halifax near the waterfront white-collar jobs increased to 96 percent of all occupations. Broader trends associated with the shift to a post-industrial economy accounted for these occupational changes, but the central area of the city attracted a disproportional number of the expanded white-collar sector. In the Halifax area as a whole such jobs rose to only 84 percent by 1996.

In Toronto the transformation of Cabbagetown into Don Vale has become a classic example of gentrification although the location lacks the natural surroundings of the inner areas of Ottawa and Halifax. A park alongside a ravine may have been an attraction in the Cabbagetown neighbourhood. It would have been more so since the old Riverdale Zoo moved away in 1974 taking its traffic and parking problems with it. For the most part, gentrifiers were attracted to Cabbagetown because of its proximity to downtown and its distinctive housing stock consisting of some of the best examples of original Victorian homes south of Bloor.

Old brick houses, some detached, gabled and trimmed with gingerbread and some terraced, flat-fronted and topped with mansard roofs, have been authentically restored and many designated and protected as heritage buildings. Compared to spacious lots in the suburbs, most Cabbagetown homes are built with narrow frontages and over the years front yards have been reduced by encroaching street widths. Gentrifiers typically fill these small yards with professionally landscaped perennial gardens and brick or stone pathways, protected from city sidewalks by wrought-iron fences. An aura of middle- and upper-class affluence permeates Cabbagetown.

Other Toronto areas of gentrification are Riverdale to the east of Cabbagetown, the western part of the old Annex, and the district between Queen and Dundas west of University Avenue.

In Toronto 52,750 less people were accommodated in the inner city in 1996 than 25 years earlier. Yet the population of the total metropolitan area including the suburbs grew by over a million-and-a-half during the same period. The loss of over 52,000 residents in the city core was remarkable in light of the appearance of 5,300 new residents in the Harbourfront area where 25 years earlier census takers found no people to count. The former high-density inner city has gone. Rooming houses that might have housed 18 to 20 people in the 1960s have almost disappeared, dropping from 1,200 in 1974 to under 400 in 1998. In their place are single-family homes rarely housing more than four people.

University-educated residents in Toronto's inner city grew as in other gentrified cities. Managerial, professional, and other white-collar occupations became the predominant type of occupation held. In areas with the most marked increase in educational and occupational levels, household incomes also pushed upward relative to those in Toronto as a whole. In Cabbagetown, for example, the average household income in 1971 was 25 percent lower than the average household income for the whole of Toronto; in 1996 its average household income was 38 percent *higher* than the city average.

While the central areas of Toronto, Ottawa, and Halifax showed significant upgrading by the late 1970s and early 1980s, redevelopment in Montreal was slower. By the 1990s, however, gentrification in Quebec's largest urban centre was an acknowledged trend. And given Montreal's advantage in being one of Canada's oldest cities, a supply of unique historical housing was available for creative gentrifiers to restore, renovate, or replicate. In some areas a mixture of all three methods was used.

Old areas of lower Westmount, developed as one of the street railway suburbs of the late 19th century, have seen a gradual influx of middle-income residents buying or renting restored premises. On streets in the area between Ste-Catherine and Ville-Marie long stretches of old attached houses have taken on a new face. Brick has been blasted and restored, late Victorian trim and cornices stripped and salvaged, and turn-of-the-century stained-glass windows given emphasis again rather than short shrift. High narrow exteriors with vertical lines giving the appearance of side-by-side houses hide interiors which are, in fact, horizontal apartments, a characteristic feature of many older Montreal residential areas. In fact, many Montrealers have traditionally preferred renting to home ownership. In Toronto, Ottawa, Vancouver, and Halifax the majority of city dwellers (roughly 58 percent) own their homes; in Montreal, by contrast, the majority rent. Homeowners represent only 48 percent of the total in Montreal.

At the far south of lower Westmount new middle-class residents have restored the "old CPR houses" on Maisonneuve adjacent to the boarded-up Westmount railway station of past years. In adjacent Shaughnessy Village to the east of lower Westmount, on streets like

Baile and Tupper, entire blocks of terrace housing built of stone have been restored. In Notre-Dame-de-Grâce, an area almost as old, a new look has been given to streets with a mixture of upgraded single-family homes and row housing.

East of the mountain, streets near Parc Lafontaine have also been revitalized. Boyer, St-Hubert and others in an area known as Plateau Mont-Royal are lined with restored three-storey row houses with, in most cases, the original outside staircases. Old wrought-iron fences have reclaimed their original function with the addition of front gardens at the street and brick or stone walkways. In this area and west to St-Denis private landlords often occupy one of their own horizontal apartments.

Another Montreal district discovered by middle-class gentrifiers is made up of the streets north of Maison Radio-Canada. Here the restoration of old row houses on streets like Wolfe and Dalcourt has taken place alongside recent construction of condominiums. In this mixture the new architecturally designed condominium buildings have faithfully replicated the row-house effect of older housing. Further west the restoration of Old Montreal increasingly includes condominiums, both in historic buildings, including old warehouses, and in new construction.

Between 1971 and 1996 the inner city of Montreal lost accommodation for over 200,000 residents, almost entirely single adults. Families have fared better. The pre-1971 family population has maintained its size though the families themselves belong to a new generation.

Middle-class families have changed the inner city profile over 25 years in as marked a manner as in Ottawa, Halifax, and Toronto. The proportion of inner city adults with university degrees has grown, overtaking the traditionally higher proportion in the suburbs. Occupations have shifted from predominantly blue-collar to predominantly white-collar. White-collar jobs in the Plateau Mont-Royal area, for example, grew from 37 percent of all jobs held by area residents in 1971 to 94 percent in 1996. University completion grew from three percent of adults to over a half.

In Vancouver inner city changes have followed a different pattern, dictated by the limits of the city's geography and city planning policies. In contrast to the developments in Ottawa, Toronto, Halifax, and Montreal, inner city areas in Vancouver have actually increased in density as city planners in the 1960s and 1970s attempted to deal with an escalating demand for housing and a shrinking land base. Policies of densification of housing within the city's boundaries were specifically chosen over the alternative of urban sprawl.

Kitsilano, with the attraction of beaches on English Bay and a view of the mountains to the north, became one of the early areas of redevelopment. In the 1970s Kitsilano was the scene of rapid demolition of older housing replaced by apartment units, both rental and condominiums, as an increasing number of Vancouver residents chose to live closer to downtown. Townhouse development followed and, in an area zoned for single-family housing, restoration of some of the old houses built before the turn of the century.

By the mid-1970s redevelopment also began further east in Fairview, an old working-class neighbourhood on the steep hill overlooking False Creek. Today in a 16-block area of townhouses, striking examples of postmodern architecture, Fairview's topography offers a view of the waterfront, the Expo site, and the mountains. Grandview-Woodland, one of Vancouver's first streetcar suburbs in the 1890s, also became an area of redevelopment in the 1970s. South of Burrard Inlet, between Clark Drive and Nanaimo Street, it lost 170 single-family housing units through demolition by the late 1970s and its stock of multiple dwelling units rose by 27 percent. Grandview-Woodland today contains a mixture of restored wood-frame houses, new townhouses, and low-rise apartments.

The trend in Vancouver's inner city toward condominium development or conversion—and toward new construction of townhouses—has had the result of keeping density high. While the other four cities lost a total of almost 300,000 residents from their central areas between 1971 and 1996, the population of Vancouver's central area increased by 46,000 during the same period. New residents, however, showed a dramatically different profile than those of 25 years earlier.

The proportion with university completion rose. In the False Creek area, for example, university graduates grew from five percent of the adult population to almost half. The more highly educated inner city population also held far different jobs in 1996 than those held by earlier residents. In the False Creek and Kitsilano areas white-collar jobs grew to 93 percent. With rising levels of education and occupation, household incomes also rose. False Creek showed the greatest change. Its incomes were, on average, 44 percent *below* the Vancouver average in 1971. In 1996 they were 12 percent *above* the average for the city.

The loss of accommodation in the central areas of Canada's major cities—accompanied by a net population loss of roughly 250,000 in five cities alone—has implications for low-income tenants who have traditionally looked for rooms or apartments in the inner city. Low vacancy rates have persisted in Ottawa and Toronto over the past two decades. Even though a tight housing market in Halifax in the 1980s has since eased, vacancies at the low end of the market are scarce. Vancouver, despite city planning policies of multiple-unit development in the 1980s, still had a bleak vacancy rate of 0.8 percent in 1994. Without vacancies, especially affordable vacancies, the number of men, women, and children looking for beds at "temporary" housing shelters rises and, in many cities, beds cannot be provided for all who are looking.

In gentrified areas of inner cities the poor are no longer being displaced. They were squeezed out ten, 15, and 20 years ago. They made their homes and raised their families in old housing that has since been fashionably upgraded and, once out of our sight, they are now out of our minds. A whole new generation of the poor, however, have never lived in the inner city at all. They are not "former" residents nor "displaced" residents; they are simply potential shelter-seekers whose housing needs cannot be met in a new middle-class inner city. Moreover, without too much thought we have poured another large group of shelter-seekers into their midst as a result of policies aimed at more effective rehabilitation of the mentally ill. These well-intentioned policies of the last quarter-century may have aimed at a better world but they have clearly missed the mark.

CHAPTER 4

Confined for Their Own Good

It is clear that long-standing social trends can be reversed. Early family formation, for example, or a predominantly industrial workforce or middle-class migration to the suburbs can all be reversed. As each social drama unfolds we are part of the cast, so preoccupied with our own roles that trends become established before we even notice their beginnings.

Far from simply demonstrating that earlier trends can shift direction, inner city social changes have had substantial consequences, chief among them the crisis of homelessness. Moreover, to stay with the social drama analogy, the plot has thickened. At the same time as middle-class migration back into the inner city has had its impact, another trend reversal has made the crisis worse. Society's mentally ill, for over a century treated in institutions, have been gradually returned to the community where, according to the best medical expertise, they will do better. As they join the ranks of the homeless in the city they must wonder what they have done to deserve this latest cruelty cloaked in kindness. While we look at the damage after a quarter of a century, it may be productive to trace the steps that have brought the mentally ill to their present situation. Over the years they have had their ups and downs.

In reviewing the various ways the mentally ill have been treated over a long period of history, it is worth recalling the limited knowledge base of this particular field within the medical profession and, of course, in the larger society until well into the 20th century. This was true in Canada and elsewhere. It is tempting to rewrite history and attribute earlier methods of treating mental illness to cruel motives. Society's response to the problem in past centuries, in fact, grew more humane along the way and many of the methods we deplore in retrospect were well-intentioned. The whole early history of the mentally ill reads like a Shakespearean tragedy, but no part of it is any more tragic than the treatment they received in the 20th century. Still lacking full knowledge of causes, we made fewer advances in providing, at a minimum, more humane treatment. We became preoccupied with economies that led to overcrowding and understaffing of facilities. Then when warehousing and custodial care of the mentally ill resulted, we implemented further economies by putting them on the streets, a form of cruelty that future generations may not be so willing to rewrite for us.

The recorded history of mental illness and its treatment goes as far back as the 14th century in England when, according to medical historian Patricia Allderidge, there is evidence that the insane were often regarded as part of the sick of all categories to be treated in hospitals. England's Holy Trinity Hospital, for example, stated in its deed that within its walls "the hungry are fed, the thirsty have drink, the naked are clothed, the sick are comforted, the dead are buried, the mad are kept safe until they are restored to reason ..." The number of insane in medieval hospitals, however, was not large. Most were cared for *outside* hospitals by family, relatives, or friends. Under English common law, such caregivers were allowed "without breach of the peace" to take a dangerously insane person and "put him into an house, to bind or chain him, and to beat him with rods, and to do any other forcible act to reclaim him, or to keep him so as he shall do no hurt." Beating with rods, it should be added, was considered one of the appropriate remedies for insanity at the time and was not necessarily considered as a punishment. The patient, however, was rarely given the opportunity to permit or refuse treatment.

If these and other acceptable measures were not effective, families in England could apply for the confinement of a dangerously insane relative in the local jail for their loved one's own safety or, more often, for the safety of the family and the community. Just as unwelcome in the local jail as at home, the difficult-to-handle mentally ill were not always accepted for admission. Family caregivers soon learned the proper wording in petitioning to have them locked up, considerable weight being attached to the risk of the mad person setting fire to themselves or their home. According to common law, a man who could be put away was typically "a man that is mad or frantic (who being at liberty attempteth to burn a house, or to do some other mischief, or to hurt himself or others ...)." At the same time the non-disruptive mentally ill were usually cared for at home unless their condition deteriorated and required outside help. The total population of mentally ill, therefore, was divided between hospital, home, and jail in the Middle Ages, with the majority very likely being cared for at home.

By the early 17th century the first English poor law required local parishes to take responsibility for their poor, among whom were listed vagrants, beggars, lunatics, and idiots, as well as the able-bodied unemployed. This requirement pushed many authorities into creating workhouses with the aim of putting employables to work or terrorizing them into finding their own work locally without delay. In this scheme of things the mentally ill were also placed in workhouses. They were required to take part in work projects if they were capable (these were the lucky ones), but since many were incapable they were simply fed and sheltered, their unruly behaviour usually restrained by chains or other means of control.

In Canada poor laws were introduced in New Brunswick and Nova Scotia when they became separate colonies in the late 18th century. In the early days, however, it would have been hard to distinguish between the poor and the settlers as they eked out their living on the land. There was no question of allocating scarce financial resources to building or operating a workhouse. As in England before workhouses, the mentally ill who could not be cared for at home were locked up in local jails. Poorhouses for the aged and infirm came later (and workhouses later still) as urban centres appeared and, in places like Saint John and Halifax, they became another option if a secure place was needed. A typical example was the Halifax Poors' Asylum, a poorhouse supported by the province and the city, where 44 insane men and women were cared for by the 1840s in what was called the "lunatic ward." In both the jail and the poorhouse the mentally ill of the Atlantic region were given custodial care only and the disruptive cases were often placed in some kind of mechanical restraint. There is no record of the kind of care given in private homes. According to one early historian, care was given at home "in what way can be imagined."[1] Certainly the permissive provisions of English common law still applied.

Upper Canada coped with its mentally ill population in a similar way, with only minor variations. Because the poor law was never adopted by the province, workhouses were not an option until the 1840s when some were operated privately, and even by the time of Confederation only four were in existence. Local jails were almost the only resource. In most communities they were established soon after the province was created although, with limited local revenues, many were poorly constructed. Jails were required by provincial statute to take in needy persons (who might otherwise have been placed in workhouses) and the insane. As a result, jail terms for the mentally ill who were dangerous, and family care at home for those who were not, were the two principal methods of treating the mentally ill in the new province. In a fewer number of cases, the mentally ill were placed in private homes in the community at a cost to ratepayers. A Middlesex County Quarter Sessions Court, for example, advanced the sum of 25 pounds to one John Barclay "for the maintenance of Janet McBean" who was deemed both insane and destitute. And in Beckwith township an Anglican clergyman who had taken in a Mrs. Nesbitt ("insane for years," it was claimed) was granted ten dollars for temporary assistance by the local council.[2]

During the same period of early settlement in Upper Canada, Lower Canada continued to treat its mentally ill as it had in New France for over 100 years. A system of *hôpitals généraux* which had spread to the colony from France in the early years housed the insane as well as the helpless poor, the aged, and the infirm. Despite their name, the *hôpitals généraux* were non-medical institutions very similar to the almshouses, poorhouses, and workhouses of England, though operated by religious orders or private individuals rather than by the government.

By the 1830s the inadequate treatment of the mentally ill in the jails, workhouses, and private homes of the Maritime region, Upper Canada, and Lower Canada demanded the attention of some, but not all, governments. For ten successive years the problem came before the Legislature of Upper Canada. Families who were having difficulty caring for a member with a mental disorder and local magistrates who were faced with overcrowded and unhealthy jail conditions were responsible for the pressure. The magistrates of the District of Ottawa, for example, stated in a petition to the province:

> That for a number of years past, the peace of the said District has been repeatedly disturbed and the moral feelings of its inhabitants shocked, by the appearances among them of maniacs, and insane persons ... [and] that although the magistrates have, in every case promptly interfered, both to protect the public, and to secure the unfortunate beings in question, yet their measures have been unavoidably attended with great public expense and inconvenience, owing to the necessity of confining and maintaining the deranged persons in the Common Gaol of the District.[3]

In Lower Canada the religious orders caring for the mentally ill in *hôpitals généraux* found it increasingly difficult to cope as numbers grew and space diminished. During the 1820s and 1830s grand juries, following their semi-annual visits, and other inquiry committees made regular representation to the provincial government about the unfitness of the buildings used for *hôpitals généraux* and the poor treatment of the mentally ill they housed. There were also 52 mentally ill inmates in the Montreal jail living in deplorable conditions and seven in a nunnery at Trois-Rivières who reportedly had been kept for years fastened to staples driven into the floors of their cells.

In New Brunswick the mentally ill in county institutions, both jails and workhouses, had increased to the point where local justices of the peace, especially the justices for the County of Saint John, demanded action from the House of Assembly. In PEI, after a decade of piecemeal grants, concern was raised about the growing expense of providing for the mentally ill on an individual case basis. A member of the Legislature for Queen's County asked for a special committee to inquire into permanent provisions for the mentally ill in light of the expense and "the melancholy situation of such unfortunate persons."[4]

The first province to act was New Brunswick. In 1835 a draft bill to establish a provincial lunatic asylum was prepared and, even as it worked its way through the Legislature, a temporary asylum was set up in Saint John on Leinster Street in an old hospital no longer in use. Opened the same year, it was the first institution specifically for the insane in Canada. With supervision by the overseer of the poor for Saint John and professional care by a visiting medical officer, the new asylum admitted 31 inmates in the first year. Over the next 12 years, it was later reported, six of the original number were discharged cured, five were discharged showing improvement, two were discharged to friends, not improved, and four had died. Of the remaining 14 transferred to a new permanent asylum, one was much improved, two perceptively improved, and 11 without visible improvement.

Though 31 mentally ill patients were accommodated in the temporary asylum, a provincial commission estimated the number in the province needing care to be 130 (or one in every 1,000 of the population). Negotiations took place with both Nova Scotia and Prince Edward Island for a joint venture to accommodate the mentally ill of all three provinces, but in the end there was no agreement. PEI had already begun construction of a provincial asylum and Nova Scotia decided a joint venture would be unworkable. New Brunswick proceeded on its own with a permanent asylum erected on 40 acres less than a mile outside Saint John. It was ready by late 1848 when 90 patients were transferred from the old temporary asylum.

Prince Edward Island had indeed established its own asylum by the time the New Brunswick patients had moved into their permanent home. A new building designed to accommodate about 20 inmates was put up on 10 acres on the York River about a mile from Charlottetown. From the outset the PEI asylum was intended not only for "insane persons" but also for "other objects of charity" as the poor were called in the legislation. The decision to combine the two groups under one roof was only one small step from the situation in the jail where they had been housed with criminals. Still, given PEI's small population of roughly 70,000 in the mid-19th century, the combined poorhouse/asylum was perhaps understandable. In fact, for PEI it was a major financial undertaking and would not have been possible had the province not recently realized 1,200 pounds from the sale of Crown lands. Twenty years later poorhouse inmates were transferred to another facility and the poorhouse/asylum became an asylum only. The separation was a small step forward for the mentally ill, but little improvement for the rest of the poor.

After deciding against the joint venture proposed by New Brunswick, Nova Scotia also moved ahead with its own plans for an asylum for the mentally ill. Several committees and commissions undertook inquiries and produced reports over the next five years, all with the goal of providing the most up-to-date asylum for Nova Scotia's mentally ill population which was estimated to be 350. The House of Assembly was urged to avoid an asylum that was "cheaply constructed or cheaply managed." Expert advice had convinced one of the inquiry committees that if it was worthwhile to have an institution, it was worthwhile to have one that would give the best possible treatment for the mentally ill.

Pleas for high standards may have been partly responsible for the delay of ten years before construction began. During the period before the first phase was completed Nova Scotia continued to accommodate the dangerous mentally ill in the Halifax poorhouse or sent whatever numbers could be admitted to the newly built New Brunswick asylum. In 1857 18 patients were received in the new Nova Scotia asylum, 13 of them transferred from the poorhouse in Halifax. The building was to accommodate 90 when it was finished.

Progress was also slow in Lower Canada. It would be difficult to overstate the pressure put on the government in the 1820s for more humane conditions for the mentally ill in Lower Canada's privately operated institutions. The final report of the special house committee was lengthy and strongly worded. After describing the cells, no greater than eight feet by seven feet, for the insane in the *hôpitals généraux* at Quebec, Montreal, and Trois-Rivières, the committee commented:

> They are simply places of confinement, without the possibility of beneficial effect upon the unhappy persons afflicted... Indeed they rather resemble places for criminals...and are more likely to produce or increase insanity than to cure it.[5]

In their final resolutions, the committee urged "that humanity loudly calls for the establishment of a lunatic asylum for the whole province."

Grand jury reports were just as critical, but 20 years elapsed before action was taken at the insistence of the Governor General of the new united province of Upper and Lower Canada. In 1845 the mentally ill of two *hôpitals généraux* (the Montreal institution no longer cared for the insane) were moved to new facilities at Beauport under new direction, an arrangement that was to be temporary until a permanent asylum was ready. Among the 23 mentally ill who arrived at the new facility from Quebec was a man who had been confined for 28 years. Barefoot for almost 20 of those years, he had been outfitted with new shoes for the trip to Beauport. In the following days seven mentally ill arrived from the *hôpital général* at Trois-Rivières and 52 from the Montreal jail which had obviously been taking in the mentally ill who would have formerly been accommodated at the Montreal *hôpital*. By 1850 the Quebec Lunatic Asylum in St. Roch parish was ready and 130 patients moved to their new home. Overcrowding began almost immediately, forcing the province to enter into new contracts with private operators, a total of five in existence by the end of the century.

In Ontario the urgency of providing an asylum for the mentally ill who were crowded into jails led finally to legislation in 1839. As a temporary measure the old York jail, then empty, was immediately repainted inside and fitted up to take in 17 patients in Toronto. Within a short time, however, the space was inadequate and other temporary quarters were opened until a permanent institution, the Provincial Lunatic Asylum, was finally opened in 1850, taking in 211 patients. In short order, overcrowding led to the opening of two new branches of the Toronto asylum over the next ten years. During the same decade the Rockwood asylum at Kingston was also opened. By the end of the century five more provincial asylums were added.

Out West mental illness was not a major problem among the sparse population in pre-Confederation years. After 1870 a small number, usually no more than three or four at any one time, were accommodated in the new Manitoba penitentiary set up at Lower Fort Garry. Only the dangerously insane were confined. By the 1880s, however, the numbers confined had grown dramatically, largely the result of the growth of the urban population at Winnipeg and new legislation that separated the mentally ill from the criminal population of the penitentiary. A new asylum, opened in 1886 at Selkirk, was designed to accommodate 167 patients and, within four years, it was filled. Another opened in Portage la Prairie in 1890. In the period around the turn of the century mentally ill of the North-West Territories, almost 100 in total, were also cared for in the two Manitoba asylums.

Saskatchewan and Alberta, separate provinces by 1905, were faced with the need for asylums for the insane over the next five years. At Ponoka in Alberta and at North Battleford in Saskatchewan institutions were established before World War I, the asylum in Saskatchewan opening with a capacity of 500, the majority of whom were transferred from the Brandon asylum in Manitoba.

In British Columbia, more settled than the Prairies in the last half of the 19th century, the old Royal Hospital in Victoria was remodelled and made into an asylum for the insane in 1873. Originally seven patients were admitted. The steady growth in the number of patients to 37 over the next four years led to the erection of a new building in New Westminster and the transfer of patients from the old Victoria hospital. Overcrowding started immediately, requiring the construction of new wings. By the end of the century the asylum had 250 patients; by 1908, over 500. With no more room for expansion, the province began the process of planning for a new mental hospital at Coquitlam to accommodate 1,800 patients.

By the early 20th century there were institutions for the insane in every province of Canada. Superintending an asylum for the insane became a growing occupation. Doctors hired as medical superintendents were often reformers with optimistic views of what could be accomplished in the new asylums. The design of buildings and grounds was an important preoccupation, but given the infancy of asylum development in both Europe and North America at mid-19th century, actual experience in treating mentally ill patients was very limited. Advances in housing the mentally ill and advances in treatment had to grow side by side.

It would seem logical to assume that the developing field of psychiatry in the 19th century gave birth to asylums for the insane but, in fact, quite the reverse was true, especially in North America. In the first quarter of the century, psychiatry was not yet an established branch of medicine. It was a limited field, struggling for legitimacy. The pressure for asylums came from those responsible for the poor, and certainly from families who could not cope with care at home. But when provincial or colonial governments became convinced that the mentally ill needed much more than the custodial care provided in jails, poorhouses, workhouses, and private homes, their officials were only slightly less knowledgeable about the causes of insanity than the medical profession. And, aside from a belief that there had to be something better for the insane than the care they were currently receiving, neither officials nor doctors knew what form that better treatment should take.

In England and in France changes in treatment of the insane had already started to take place. Two medical reformers, in particular, were noted for new approaches to treatment, more humane approaches which they had both introduced separately in their respective countries. William Tuke in England and Philippe Pinel in France had both become known for removing the chains of the insane and giving, in their place, kindness and respect. More specifically, in day-to-day treatment they emphasized physical exercise, fresh air, good diet, and employment (as in today's occupational therapy). Most of the violent mentally ill had responded well when chains were removed, and humanitarian methods soon spread to asylums throughout England and continental Europe.

The methods of Tuke and Pinel were copied in many American asylums by the 1820s. News of their innovations also found its way to Canada and especially to those looking into new ways to provide for the mentally ill. In 1824 the house committee studying the feasibility of an insane asylum for Lower Canada, its first, was instructed that the asylum should be "adapted to the improved modern system of treatment for the insane." By the 1830s, when the New Brunswick asylum was in the planning stages, commissioners appointed to make inquiries abroad reported back that the severe discipline of former times had given way to a system whose chief characteristics were kindness and mildness. They quoted the comments of a Glasgow asylum superintendent:

> ...we have no machinery; we neither drown nor torture them into reason; we meet them as friends and brothers, cultivate their affections, interest their feelings, rouse their attention, and excite their hopes.[6]

In the same vein the medical superintendent of Ontario's asylum for the insane gave assurance in his first annual report that he was against the use of mechanical restraints for patients and in favour of fresh air and exercise which made the use of restraints largely unnecessary. But more exercise space was badly needed, he added. While waiting for a better-equipped permanent asylum he had been sending patients out to fish in the Toronto bay.

The application of humanitarian methods in treating the insane was not based on any breakthrough in discovering the causes of insanity. It was true that the new approach rejected, among other things, the old treatment of bloodletting and, with it, the theory that an overabundance of blood inflamed the brain causing severe disorganization, or insanity. But no new theories arose in its place. If anything, the shift to more humane treatment (which was actually called "moral treatment") was based on fresh opinions that medical treatment of any kind was not working with the mentally ill. Instead what was needed was to develop the self-reliance and self-control of patients, to encourage them to accept responsibility for their actions, and to reward appropriate personal behaviour.

While this became the predominant outlook when asylums for the insane were established in Canada after the 1840s, there was much backsliding throughout the remainder of the century. No sooner were provincial asylums opened when they were seriously overcrowded. As space and staff diminished in relation to the number of patients, old methods of caring for the mentally ill were more frequently used. The crowded temporary quarters used for Toronto's mentally ill in the 1840s were an early example. After four years of operation a visitor reported that the old treatment of bleeding patients was being used and that most of the 70 patients looked emaciated and wretched from lack of food. Meat especially was not allowed.

In Quebec the system of contracting-out asylum care continued throughout the century. Private organizations, often religious orders, operated asylums and were paid approximately $175 a year per patient. The inherent need for economy in this system led to abuses. One inspector reported as early as 1864 that following the expansion of one asylum to relieve overcrowding, he was surprised to observe that "even while the works were advancing" the proprietors made continued additions to the number of patients. He went on:

> The thought then began to be forced on me, that the interests of the lunatics, their health and comfort, were of secondary consideration throughout. The Proprietors give their assurance of their having informed the Government that their Institution is and has been much over-populated, and I have no reason, of course to doubt the assurance, and it may have been with great compunction that physicians, who know the effects upon lunatics of congregating them at night in cribs erected in badly ventilated rooms, under such circumstances, consented to what, as professional men, they condemned.[7]

In British Columbia space in the old hospital in Victoria was pushed to the limit soon after its opening as patients increased from 16 to 37 without expansion of the building. To keep order, staff resorted to the use of mechanical restraint. In the Rockwood asylum at Kingston a new medical superintendent arriving in 1878 (13 years after its opening) found restraint used with nearly ten percent of the patients.

Admissions continued to flood BC's asylum after it was moved to the mainland. In New Westminster overcrowding started almost the day of opening. The 37 patients transferred from Victoria more than filled the 28 single rooms and within a year the number had increased to 49, forcing staff to fill corridors, sitting rooms, and clothes rooms with beds. Though new wings were added the superintendent also complained about a shortage of staff throughout the 1880s. Finally in 1894 charges of ill-treatment of patients and excessive use of restraint were made against the asylum. An investigation by a royal commission found the charges to be well-founded. Patients were reported to be sleeping with their hands in handcuffs behind them for many nights. Other unusually severe methods were also being used.

In PEI a new asylum built in 1879 was so overcrowded ten years later that the living quarters of the medical superintendent had to be used for patients and, as a result, the superintendent became a visiting medical officer. The relief of overcrowding, however, was only temporary. Within a few years the medical officer reported that in the overcrowded state of the asylum it was impossible to dispense with mechanical restraint and impossible to institute a program of employment therapy for patients.

The commitment to a more humane method of treating the mentally ill was slowly eroding. Overcrowding was the most significant contributing factor. Buildings were originally designed with bed capacities that would allow the transfer of the mentally ill who had been inadequately accommodated for years in jails and workhouses. But there were soon other demands on beds. General population growth accounted for some of the rapid increase in admissions that overwhelmed new asylums as soon as they opened. In addition, the very existence of facilities for the mentally ill created a trend toward institutional care or, more importantly, a social acceptance of institutional care that had not been part of 19th-century thinking before. As long as there were asylums, they were put to use by families who might earlier have tried to manage at home.

Asylum planning had also been based on overly optimistic estimates of discharge rates that would allow new admissions to be absorbed. Though many moderately ill patients responded to the "moral treatment" applied and had short institutional stays, still more were severe chronic cases who were hopelessly beyond treatment. Chronic incurable cases bottlenecked the whole admission-and-discharge process and soon left less and less capacity in asylums for patients who might respond to treatment. Pressure from medical superintendents and the public usually produced new quarters, but they were inadequate to meet the demand by the time they were ready. Superintendents who had been so optimistic about the effectiveness of humane treatment became disillusioned with results despite the reality that they were barely able to put a humane philosophy into practice. By the end of the 19th century asylums for the insane began to provide custodial care only. Ultimately not much else was expected of them, a situation that showed little change for the next 50 years.

Outside the institutions the psychiatric profession grew slowly during the 20th century, showing stronger acceptance in the US than in Canada. The bleak outlook for cure of the mentally ill in insane asylums, now called mental hospitals, did not attract many to institutional work. The new psychoanalytic methods of Freud (around 1910) were initially treated with suspicion and were not used to a great extent in mental hospitals. There were breakthroughs in *physical* treatment of mental illness by the 1940s with the introduction of insulin and electric shock and brain surgery, some of which were used in mental hospitals in Canada. But for the most part mental hospitals had become warehouses, and the public and the psychiatric profession had written them off. When they were opened enthusiastically in the 1840s and 1850s they were a progressive response to the mistreatment of the mentally ill in jails and workhouses, but their methods were based on incomplete knowledge of the causes of mental illness and little in the way of medical advances came along over the next 100 years to make that knowledge more complete.

CHAPTER 5

Discharged for Their Own Good

How a good portion of the mentally ill got from the back wards of
mental hospitals to the streets is the story of a public policy run
amok. By mid-20th century governments in Britain, the US, and
Canada could no longer continue the building-and-expansion
solution to rising mental hospital populations. The timing was
fortunate. Government objectives of containing costs were
compatible with the objective of the medical profession to distance
itself from the mental hospital with its image of warehousing patients
who were not responding to medical treatment. Hand in hand,
governments and psychiatrists set out to reduce the mental hospital
population in the 1950s and 1960s. Patients would be returned to
the community—to their homes or to other residential facilities—
where they would benefit from a normal social environment that
would rehabilitate them with the help of support services
theoretically available near where they live. In the end, it would be
the long-term or chronic mentally ill patient who would frustrate
their efforts, just as the chronic patient had frustrated the humane
efforts of the 19th century.

Chronic patients historically made up half the population of
mental hospitals.[1] But it was a persistent, intractable, untreatable
half. Chronic patients were always there as a reminder that medical
solutions had not yet been found, that psychiatry could still not
claim to be totally scientific, and that successes in treating short-
term patients with non-psychotic disorders would always be offset
by failures with the long-term mentally ill. With the chronic patients
representing half, one can understand professional exasperation that

amounted to: *the mentally ill population could be completely cured if it weren't for the half that is incurable.*

Solutions for the chronic caseload problem had been sought as far back as the turn of the century. Rather than disheartening staff any further and, in fact, prolonging the pattern of failure that would eventually turn away good quality professionals, some mental hospitals in England and North America had found ways to filter incoming patients at intake. Filtering consisted of sending potentially chronic or long-term cases directly into the mental hospital, where they would very likely occupy a hospital bed for a minimum of two years, and keeping short-term cases at an intake facility where they would be given the best available treatment and hopefully would not have to enter the hospital at all. It was clearly a solution that recognized that effective treatment for short-term patients was difficult within the mental hospital, given the demands on staff time and physical resources created by the immovable long-term caseload.

In the US new psychopathic hospitals established before World War I were intended to fill this function. Generally known as receiving hospitals, they acted as clearing houses referring chronic cases to public mental hospitals and, in association with medical schools, providing advanced treatment in the receiving hospital for short-term patients. If responding to treatment, patients could stay up to two, sometimes four, months. A limited number of American psychopathic hospitals were opened in the early years, among them the Boston Psychopathic Hospital, the New York State Psychiatric Institute, and Bellevue. In England the Maudsley Hospital was conceived by a former medical superintendent with 50 years' first-hand experience with the build-up of chronic cases in mental hospitals. The hospital, built in 1915, gave short-term treatment to early and acute cases of mental illness and provided a teaching and research function for the University of London.

Even earlier a number of reception wards were set up in Canada in connection with four mental hospitals in Ontario. With the main purpose of admitting and treating short-term cases, reception wards served the Rockwood Asylum at Kingston, and asylums at Toronto, London, and Brockville. The earliest two were the reception wards at Rockwood opened in 1894 and Toronto opened in 1907, both created by Dr. C.K. Clarke who was later instrumental in establishing the Toronto Psychiatric Hospital. With the same function as the psychopathic hospitals in the US and the Maudsley in England, the Toronto Psychiatric Hospital was closely linked with the university medical school. By 1919 a psychopathic ward was also in operation in the Winnipeg General Hospital, receiving patients who formerly would have been placed in jails while waiting for placement in Manitoba's mental hospitals.

Besides filtering to keep short-term cases from entering the mental hospital, procedures were also introduced to move long-term cases out. Early in the 1930s residential care was provided for chronic patients in Ontario in what were called approved homes. The homes were actually supervised by provincial hospital staff, and long-term patients who were considered harmless were transferred into a boarding-out situation though remaining on the hospital books.

While filtering through reception hospitals and placement in approved homes were intended to reduce the mental hospital population, there were only a small number of these innovations in Canada. They barely made a dent on the never-ending flow of admissions of both short- and long-term patients into institutions across the country. In 1930 provincial mental institutions in Canada accommodated approximately 30,000 patients. In 1940, long after the introduction of reception (or psychopathic) hospitals and approved homes, they accommodated 44,000. Moreover, during the Depression decade all expansion of physical space stopped. The 44,000 patients at the end of the Depression were cared for in facilities with a total bed capacity of 39,000. Admissions were high, and discharges sluggish. Of the total mental hospital population, the proportion of chronic long-term cases remained steady.

New treatments were introduced in the late 1930s, some targeting the previously untreatable chronic patient. All were used in the Toronto Psychiatric Hospital and some were used in other provincial mental hospitals across Canada. Insulin coma therapy, discovered in Germany, was first used in the US in 1936 and in Canada in 1937, first at the provincial hospital in New Toronto, Ontario, and within a year at provincial hospitals in Saint John, New Brunswick, and Verdun, Quebec. One two-year research study involved insulin therapy treatment of schizophrenic patients. A year later schizophrenic patients were also the subjects of Metrazol shock therapy when it was introduced in Canadian mental hospitals. Over the next few years Metrazol became one of the commonest of shock therapies used. For patients with major depression, and indeed for schizophrenic patients as well, electroshock therapy was introduced in Canada in 1941 and replaced Metrazol to a great extent. Lobotomy was also a treatment of the 1940s although it became more popular later. Overcrowding at mental hospitals continued to place pressure on psychiatrists to try these new treatments. As each new therapy became available it was enthusiastically adopted, tending to replace earlier innovations that had failed to measure up to optimistic claims. Although the mental hospital population in Canada still continued to grow over the next ten years despite the new treatments, the increase of 10,000 patients was only 22 percent compared to the 47 percent increase during the Depression decade. And while everything from insulin therapy to lobotomy had been tried, the proportion of chronic patients showed no change.

The 22 percent increase was still not low enough to satisfy those responsible for provincial budgets. At the same time federal government officials, reportedly shocked by recent figures that showed that over 40 percent of all hospital beds in the country were occupied by the mentally ill, decided to act. A program of National Health Grants was introduced, providing funds to the provinces for surveys of existing mental health services and future needs. Out of these surveys and several interprovincial meetings of health ministers came federal funding for expansion of mental hospital beds and for a variety of new approaches to mental health care, chief among them an offer of funding for the construction (and operation, in some cases) of community mental health centres and psychiatric units within general hospitals. The new approaches were intended to reduce mental hospital populations by early treatment of acute cases in local communities. In the 1950s the provinces, even as they applied for federal grants to expand the old mental hospitals, began to turn in the direction of the new community-based options for the location of treatment and care of the mentally ill.

Different provinces chose different ways of using federal funds and their own funds to experiment with a shift toward community care. In Nova Scotia a federal grant went toward the creation of a community mental health centre at Wolfville in 1955 to serve the counties of Kings, West Hants, and Annapolis. The centre's services were based on the principle that the treatment of mental illness had a greater chance of success if provided early and close to home with local community support. The staff of the mental health centre at Wolfville, closely affiliated with Acadia University, included a psychiatrist, a psychiatric social worker, and a psychologist, a staff complement that became the model for six other community mental health centres created over the next seven years in Nova Scotia, all funded under federal mental health grants with provincial cost-sharing. Federal-provincial grants sponsored similar centres across the country in the 1950s.

With the same goal of reducing reliance on long-term mental hospital care, Ontario moved in another direction. Even before federal grants were introduced in 1948, the provincial government had established two psychiatric units in general hospitals—at Ottawa's Civic Hospital and London's Victoria Hospital. Twenty-two beds were provided in these units. Following implementation of the national grants program, a 32-bed unit was created at the Toronto General with federal funding. More funds were made available in the early 1950s in the amount of $1,500 for each chronic psychiatric bed in general hospitals. Acting on this federal offer, Minister of Health Mackinnon Phillips announced a new mental health policy for Ontario—new psychiatric units would be established in general hospitals across the province, allowing for early treatment of mental illness with the objective of making admission to a mental hospital unnecessary. By 1958 over 350 psychiatric beds were available in hospital units in Ontario.

In Saskatchewan, the government's psychiatric services branch developed a plan in the early 1950s to replace its two large mental hospitals at Weyburn and North Battleford with eight small regional hospitals accommodating no more than 300 patients each. Because its regional thrust represented a shift away from the large distant mental hospitals of the past, the plan received considerable attention outside the province, but there were delays in receiving government approval. In the meantime, funds (both federal and provincial) were directed at psychiatric units in general hospitals to serve some of the regions identified in the plan. A 39-bed psychiatric ward in the University Hospital, Saskatoon, was in operation by 1955; a 24-bed unit opened in Moose Jaw in 1956; and an older 20-bed unit at the Regina General Hospital was expanded. Despite these commitments to new wards in general hospitals, Saskatchewan's earlier plan for small mental hospitals was not dead. Once approved, planning went ahead with the first of these, the Yorkton Psychiatric Centre, to be opened in the 1960s. So Saskatchewan was experimenting with both community-based alternatives, small mental hospitals, and psychiatric wards in general hospitals, and by the late 1950s it had still not decided which way to go.

In 1950 British Columbia was also looking for ways to stop the growth of large mental hospitals. The Crease Clinic, a provincial psychiatric hospital, was opened in that year taking voluntary admissions for the first time and providing short-term treatment in an attempt to redirect a portion of admissions that would have been destined for the provincial mental hospitals at Essondale or Colquitz. But specialized psychiatric hospitals were not the direction BC would finally take. By the end of the decade funds had gone to 64 beds in the psychiatric units of two general hospitals. The province was also exploring the same model in other general hospitals and was making plans for a new community mental health centre which it hoped would be the first of many in support of the new general hospital units.

The changes brought about by large injections of new mental health funding in the 1950s were not immediately apparent in the size of the traditional caseload. Experimenting with options other than the provincial mental hospital approach was one thing, but it was quite another to undercut the dominance of the old institutions that had been the only place of care for the mentally ill for over a century. While community-based care was being tried, massive funds were still going into expansion of provincial mental hospitals across Canada. At least 80 percent of over 20,000 new beds funded under the National Health Grants went to provincial mental hospitals. By the mid-1950s the number of mental hospital patients had increased by another six percent, almost 5,000 more patients than five years earlier. But there was a bright side. Perhaps unnoticed by patients and staff in the overcrowded hospitals, the five-year increase actually represented a slowing down of growth. Beds in psychiatric units of general hospitals were still small in number, only 870 across Canada in 1956, but that number represented an increase of three times the number of psychiatric beds in 1951. Besides the units mentioned earlier (three in Ontario, three in Saskatchewan, and two in BC), two psychiatric units in general hospitals in the Atlantic provinces, eight in Quebec, two in Manitoba, two in Alberta, and six more in Ontario had also been opened. General hospitals would continue to provide a greater and greater portion of beds for the mentally ill. These were signs of change even before the 1960s when the whole distribution of the mentally ill would be dramatically turned around.

It was not enough that government mental health departments and the psychiatric profession wanted to dismantle mental hospitals. Although short-term beds in the community increased, long-term beds in the back wards of mental hospitals were still full. The hard core group seemed to be there to stay.

Other countries were grappling with the same problem. In the US state governments were also pressing for the reduction of patients in overcrowded public mental hospitals. Largely as a result of their pressure a Joint Commission on Mental Illness and Health was set up by the federal government to recommend future directions for care of the mentally ill. Among several possible solutions recommended, the United States chose community mental health centres as an alternative to care in state mental hospitals. In England community care was also being expanded. Many mental hospitals in large cities had provided outpatient clinics for over 20 years. Now local authorities began to assume responsibility for community programs to support them, including day and night hospitals for the mentally ill, sheltered workshops, and other experiments. The Mental Health Act of 1959 reinforced the orientation of services away from the mental hospital toward community care, but it was another two years before the Minister of Health announced just how that would be done. With his announcement, a new national policy of reducing mental hospital beds by half and relocating the remaining half in psychiatric units of general hospitals was put in place at once with little public awareness of the effect such a change would have on urban centres in Britain.

At the same time as the US was starting to fund community mental health centres and Britain was relocating beds to general hospitals, Canada was narrowing its choices to the general hospital solution. Despite their varying strategies, however, all three countries now had clear policies of reducing mental hospital populations and turning toward community-based care for the mentally ill. Reductions were slow at first, and dates for meeting projected targets seemed a long way off. But unexpectedly, and perhaps unfortunately, two new developments appeared in succession, each having its own impact on the discharge of patients from mental hospitals. In retrospect, the new developments were responsible for speeding up the discharge process in all three countries to such a rate that thousands of mentally ill patients were sent out before local communities were ready.

The first impact came with the introduction of chlorpromazine, the first antipsychotic medication with extraordinary results for the chronic mentally ill. Known as Thorazine, it became available in the mid-1950s. Tests began to show that Thorazine could help conditions like chronic schizophrenia, making patients easier to handle, less aggressive or hostile and, in general, acting as a powerful tranquillizer. Promoters of the new drug made no claims about its ability to cure, but the fact that it could have such a remarkable effect on symptoms made it imaginable, for the first time, to think of the chronic mentally ill managing to live outside of the hospital.

Following the introduction of antipsychotic medication the mental hospital population in the US and Britain began to drop slowly. In Canada reductions failed to materialize for another five years. As a result, a second development—the introduction of federal funds into the whole hospital equation—has been credited with the turnaround in mental hospital numbers in Canada, and there is evidence it also played a role in the US greater than the role of antipsychotic medication. Canada was slowly moving toward a system of national hospital insurance, slow because the responsibility for health rested with provincial governments and they were by no means unanimous. Under a new system, federal funding of about 50 percent was being offered with a major stipulation that provincial plans would provide universal coverage, that is, hospital insurance would be available free to all income groups. After lengthy negotiations the federal plan took effect in 1958 and over the next few years all ten provincial plans met the requirements for federal funding. In contrast to the British National Health Service, however, mental hospitals were not to be included in Canada's new health insurance program. The result was perhaps inevitable. Provincial governments recognized immediately that, out of the blue, they had a solution for meeting a good portion of their costs for the mentally ill. Beds for short-term cases would be transferred to psychiatric wards in general hospitals and would be covered by federal funding under hospital insurance for savings of millions (to provincial taxpayers). At the same time the psychiatric profession saw the shift to general hospitals as a way of providing the scientific and medical legitimacy psychiatry had always lacked.

In the US universal hospital insurance was not on either the state or federal agenda. Hospital coverage for low-income groups, however, was imminent. In 1960 the federal government introduced Medical Assistance to the Aged (Medicare) subsidizing hospital and nursing home care for low-income elderly, and in 1965 it introduced Medicaid subsidizing hospital care for the poor. Under both programs coverage did *not* include state-run mental hospitals. The new legislation allowed state governments to move 30 percent of their mental hospital caseload into nursing homes where federal funding would amount to between 50 percent and 78 percent. For the non-elderly, state governments also began to look with more favour on the option of specialized units in general hospitals which would bring in federal funding under Medicaid.

Beginning in 1965 the state mental hospital population in the US decreased steadily each year while the nursing home population grew. In Canada and Britain mental hospital patients decreased while patients in psychiatric units of general hospitals grew. (By the early 1960s roughly 70 general hospitals in Canada contained psychiatric units and 40 percent of new mental patient admissions went to these units.) Over the next 30 years these policies in all three countries led to remarkable reductions in mental hospital populations. By 1991 Britain's Department of Health had closed 60 of its psychiatric hospitals, reducing the 1955 peak of 165,000 patients by almost 75 percent. By the early 1990s patients in American and Canadian mental hospitals had also decreased by 75 percent, leaving only 80,000 in mental hospitals in the US and under 15,000 in mental hospitals in Canada.

Looking back on the 1960s and 1970s we can now see that policies of reducing mental hospital populations to a quarter of their size in less than 20 years were rash and opportunistic. But hindsight gives us an advantage. How could government officials and psychiatrists (who were often the same people) have known that chronic mental patients who had difficulty with the most basic living skills were being discharged into competitive urban environments of scarce housing and scarce jobs? How could they have known that the middle class was in the process of reclaiming the inner city, reducing the low-income housing stock, and staking its claim with zoning laws that ruled out group homes and halfway houses? It may also be understandable that officials and psychiatrists thought there were "after-care" caseworkers waiting in the community to remind the mentally ill to take their medication or to show them the way to the welfare office. Or that there were sheltered workshops and recreation programs to help them feel like human beings again.

Support services were, for the most part, non-existent. Some discharged patients managed without them, especially those discharged to their families, but the chronic mentally ill were the hardest hit. It was true that tranquillizing with the new antipsychotic drugs made them more socially acceptable. It did not, however, restore their sanity and endow them with rational thinking. Stretching their welfare allowance over a month was beyond their skill level as was what to spend it on when they had it. The antipsychotic drugs also failed to transform them into normal-looking citizens, and there were reports that some community agencies preferred to help short-term cases rather than the unkempt long-term mentally ill. In the US the staff of one community mental health centre tried to find ways of making the waiting room uninviting to chronic patients who tended to come hours or even days early for their appointments. Probably the most effective way of getting rid of chronic patients was used by an outpatient clinic in the process of relocating. A worker in adjoining premises reported:

One weekend, the staff moved the program…to its new location and deliberately avoided telling certain patients when the move was to take place and where the new clinic would be. On Monday morning, all those selected for abandonment showed up at the empty site and stood, helpless and befuddled, until someone found the courage to break the news of their betrayal.[2]

In England a survey of community outpatient programs found that patients with more serious psychiatric disorders like schizophrenia and affective psychosis were seen less often than other mentally ill patients.

Within a few years follow-up studies on discharged chronic patients began to appear. In Canada many had been discharged directly into special homes set up under new provincial legislation (as in Ontario), many had been discharged into foster homes approved specifically to receive mental hospital patients (as in Saskatchewan) or licensed boarding homes (as in BC), and many, especially the elderly, in all provinces had been transferred to nursing homes. Chronic patients also went to unlicensed commercial boarding homes. Most fell into these five non-family residential settins. Others were returned to their families, some lived in Salvation Army hostels, and a few sought accommodation on their own. Researchers found that outcomes for the chronic mentally ill varied from province to province, even city to city, depending on the availability of a range of community programs to help put the chronic patient back in society. One study found that where these programs were provided, most of the chronic mentally ill had been able to fit into homes approved for their care. In another study, homes mandated by legislation were reviewed. Without social, physical or recreational activity, schizophrenic patients in these homes tended to become slow and disoriented and to function at a much lower, more dependent level than where such activities were available. A third study found that many ex-patients were living in poor conditions in commercial boarding homes. Again the lack of after-care services like recreation facilities, vocational rehabilitation, and sheltered workshops left ex-patients with no stimulation and a bleak living environment. A Montreal study of foster homes that were recruited to provide a family environment for discharged patients found that in most cases the discharged patients had their meals separately from the foster family and were subjected to a certain amount of regimentation.

It was clear that homes used for the placement of discharged patients, even those homes requiring conformity to certain standards, had mixed reviews. Just as the mental hospitals had deteriorated to custodial care for chronic patients, residential care was in danger of falling to the same level of service. In both cases, the mentally ill fared poorly because mental illness failed to interest the public; indifference resulted in assigning it a low priority and, most certainly, the minimum amount of public funds that could be spared. Funds spent on services to help the mentally ill live in the community made the difference between a vegetative and a human existence. And these were the people with a roof over their heads!

Many of the discharged mentally ill (and a whole new generation of mentally ill treated in general hospitals rather than the old mental institutions) were unable to get regular shelter, let alone hang on to it if they did manage to get it. A tight rental market, especially in the centre of the city, left them out; their tendency to look outlandish and the likelihood that they would have difficulty meeting regular rent payments made landlords nervous. They became candidates for the hostels, the missions, and the emergency shelters. Many, of course, could not even make it in temporary shelters and ended up on the streets or in jail.

Out of roughly 44,000 patients discharged from Canadian mental hospitals between 1960 and 1990, an estimate of a quarter who could not cope in foster or boarding homes or their own rental arrangements is reasonable, given that studies have shown that 75 percent managed to fit into their living arrangements. If we add 3,000 who have developed long-term mental illness in the last 20 years (who were never part of the old mental hospital statistics), a conservative estimate is 14,000 mentally ill people among the homeless. The simple arithmetic is that the mentally ill who were expected to make it in the community but failed to do so have increased the ranks of the homeless by 50 percent. The basic problem of scarce housing—more specifically, the disappearance of low-rent housing in Canada's major cities—confronted the mentally ill just as they were being returned to the community and has confronted a new generation of mentally ill who are also expected to make it on their own. On welfare or on disability allowances, they are clearly to be counted among the poor, but surely they are the most vulnerable of the poor. So far we have fallen short of a cure for their illness. It may come some day, but in the meantime we have also fallen short of the most basic step of bringing them in from the cold.

CHAPTER 6

The Homeless: The Poorest of the Poor

For the most part the homeless in Canada are on the streets or in temporary shelters because the low end of the housing market is shrinking. Thousands of low-rent housing units have been lost through demolition, conversion, or restoration. The central neighbourhoods of five major cities, in particular, now have a predominantly middle-class profile. Rooming and boarding houses have all but disappeared; single-room occupancy hotels with low daily rates have gone out of business, either bulldozed or zoned into oblivion. The process over the past 25 years has been called gentrification and it has been a significant cause of homelessness.

But gentrification is not the whole story. There are Canadian cities with populations over 500,000 where the central core has not been transformed by an influx of middle-class gentrifiers— Edmonton, Calgary, and Winnipeg, among others. The trend is also missing in Saskatoon and Regina with populations of roughly 200,000 each. In those cities, despite losses through demolition, the central core still contains a supply of low-cost housing units. Yet emergency shelters for the homeless do a brisk business, and many live on the streets.

Other developments in the housing market provide an explanation. Inner city housing may not have changed physically in the five largest prairie cities, but it has moved out of reach of a large portion of tenants who might have been able to afford it in past years. Tragically, we have more poor Canadians than we used to have. And the gap between their incomes and the incomes of the rest of us has grown wider. Although the housing markets in non-gentrified cities like Calgary and Edmonton tightened up in the last part of the 1990s, vacancy rates were not extraordinarily low earlier when the homeless first appeared on their streets. Still, in the competition for the housing units that were available, the poorest of the poor were not even in the ballpark. As vacancy rates dropped, the situation became even worse. The construction of new housing to address these tight markets has failed to keep pace with demand, especially in the rental market. New housing starts have been heavily in favour of ownership units.

With an improving Canadian economy in the last part of the 1990s and the early part of the new century, we make mistaken assumptions about the widespread sharing of this good fortune. Faced with destitute souls on the street whose very existence is incongruous in an affluent society, we want to believe they are the authors of their own misfortune. We point to drug addiction and alcoholism (which certainly affect roughly a third of the homeless) and see them as self-inflicted deficiencies. If these people had chosen otherwise, the argument goes, they wouldn't be on the streets.

But there are obvious questions we should be asking. Who willingly would choose to sleep outdoors, or on floor mats or cots in public shelters, in Canada's weather? What benefits to such a way of life are attracting so many? Where is the pleasure in carrying with you all your belongings in a plastic bag or in a shopping cart when you might keep them safely in a room somewhere? Where is the good side of all this? We must surely be missing something. To talk about choosing such a way of life is, at best, ludicrous, and at worst, an exercise in denial. The homeless are homeless not because they choose to be, but because no other choice is open to them. They are poor—in fact, the poorest of our poor—and for over 20 years an increasing share of our population has dropped into their ranks. There were 3.6 million Canadians living in poverty in 1980; today there are over five million. This change represents an increase of 41 percent in the numbers of poor while the total Canadian population has increased by only 26 percent during the same period. Five million people means over 17 percent of Canadians are living in poverty. To turn these figures into two groups we can readily identify with, one in seven Canadian families are poor; one in three Canadian single people are poor.

These proportions are mirrored in Canada's homeless population. Singles are overrepresented among the homeless; they are also overrepresented among the poor. Statistics on the marital status of Canadians show twice as many families as singles in the general population. But the situation is reversed for those living below the poverty line where singles outnumber families by about 300,000 across the country. Poverty rates for singles are normally two-and-a-half times higher than the rates for families, an indication that two-earner families are now the norm, putting them less at risk of being counted among the poor. Singles are not only more likely to be poor, their incomes are far below the poverty line. While the poverty line itself represents a meager income level, single males live on close to half that amount. Understandably they make up the majority of the homeless in Canada. During the 1990s there were also marked increases in the number of single females showing up at emergency shelters (they were less likely than males, however, to live on the street).

There are other connections between poverty and homelessness. The rate of poverty among Canadians living in major urban centres is twice as high as among rural Canadians. Reflecting this, the majority of homeless people are concentrated in Canada's major cities. The same link shows up in income sources. Half of Canada's poor under 65 years of age are in receipt of welfare or employment insurance. More than half of the homeless are also on welfare.

These similarities are not unhappy coincidences. The homeless are not only a part of the poor, they are the most destitute of the poor. Whether middle-class gentrifiers have taken over the inner city (as in large centres) or whether the middle class is not attracted to the inner city (as in smaller centres), the most destitute of the poor have not been able to afford the lowest rents in the low end of the market. They are not choosing to be homeless. If they have a choice at all, it is to try to stay alive despite having no shelter, and certainly an increasing number are not even making that choice.

Among the most destitute, some are worse off than others. There are roughly one million Aboriginal people in the Canadian population, and most of them are poor. There are roughly one million lone parents in the Canadian population, and most of them are poor. That they have been the poorest Canadians for so many years is a testimony to public indifference. Four or five different political parties have had their turn running provincial or federal governments over the same years, but not one has felt it necessary to place these groups at the top of their agendas. Clearly politicians feel no pressure about their plight. Aboriginal people developed a stronger voice in the last part of the 20th century, but it was not sufficiently strong for anyone to listen. Lone parents, who are mostly women, have no voice at all. They are isolated from each other with little opportunity for organization. Small wonder that we do not hear from them. The extent of poverty among Aboriginal people and lone parents in Canada warrants closer inspection. It helps explain why they are overrepresented among the poor and, in turn, among the homeless and why their proportions are increasing as solutions continue to escape us.

A major group among Canada's poor is made up of the Aboriginal population. We are regularly criticized by the international community—and sometimes more formally by the United Nations—for failing to address the issue of the extreme poverty of our Native people, an issue that has been with us for many years. If the fact that 17 percent of all Canadians live below the poverty line shocks us, the fact that twice that proportion of Aboriginal people live below the poverty line may make us realize that some are bearing the brunt of poverty out of all proportion to their numbers and beyond all considerations of fairness and human rights.

In the last half-century it has become increasingly evident that national policies related to the Aboriginals have been seriously misguided since colonial years. At times policies have been based on a failure to understand Native culture. At other times they have clearly been deceitful. Nonetheless, in our treatment of Aboriginal people we dug ourselves in deeper during the 20th century, and we enter the 21st century with a better understanding of the solutions but almost complete public indifference to their implementation. The poverty of the Aboriginal population is the result of these flawed policies and our apathy about setting things right. Generally unskilled and lagging behind the rest of Canadians in educational level, it is not surprising that the unemployment rate for Aboriginal people was over 24 percent in 1991, more than two-and-a-half times that of the general population. Moreover, the gap between Aboriginal unemployment and general unemployment had widened over the ten-year period leading up to 1991. The average Aboriginal income, as a result, is less than two-thirds of the average income of non-Aboriginal Canadians. This translates into a dependence on welfare that undermines attempts to make a better future for today's young Aboriginal people.

With Aboriginal peoples making their homes in the Far North (the Inuit) and on reserves (registered Indians) and in rural communities or settlements (both registered and non-status Indians), it might seem unlikely that their poverty would surface among the homeless on urban streets. The reality is that the rural-to-urban movement of the 20th century has affected Aboriginal people as much as others. Especially during the 1960s many registered Indians moved out of reserves and many other Aboriginal people moved out of rural communities in both the North and South. Their destination was urban centres, sometimes small but for the most part large, and the greatest urban influx was into major cities of the Prairies. In 1961 urban Aboriginal people were few, only 14 percent of all Aboriginal people; over the next ten years roughly 65,000 left reserves and rural communities. By 1971 the proportion of urban Aboriginal people had jumped to 30 percent of the total and by 1981 to more than half. Although there has been migration back and forth between reserves and urban centres over the last three decades, there are large Aboriginal populations in Winnipeg, Calgary, Edmonton, Regina, and Saskatoon, showing little sign of decline.

Aboriginal people, like migrants in the general population, move to cities in search of better employment and educational opportunities. But they are more likely to move for other reasons as well, a major stimulus being housing problems. Housing conditions on reserves and in the Far North are among the worst in Canada. Houses are in poor repair, and basic services like indoor plumbing and central heating are by no means universal. In addition, Aboriginal households are larger than the average Canadian household, while their houses are smaller, resulting in overcrowding that sends many in search of better accommodation in the city.

Despite their hopes for improved conditions after migration, Aboriginal people who now live in large urban centres generally live in inadequate housing measured by the most basic standards. In most prairie cities inner city housing is not new, a substantial majority of units built before World War II. As a result, an estimated quarter of this old housing has deteriorated to the point where neighbourhoods are considered to be in a stage of decline. In this setting over half of Aboriginal people live in housing that needs repair. But they have little choice. The majority of those who moved into Winnipeg, Regina, Saskatoon, and Edmonton in the 1990s have incomes below the poverty line. Moreover, given their lack of access to capital, Aboriginal people are renters rather than owners (62 percent compared to 43 percent for the rest of Canadians). Even the most inadequate housing in the inner city is at rents beyond their individual or family budgets, and they regularly experience housing problems that cause them to move. Aboriginal people move within cities at a far greater rate than the rest of the population (almost three-quarters of Winnipeg's Aboriginal population made at least one move during a five-year period); in most cities they move almost twice as often as the remaining population. As surveys have shown for all Canadians, the majority of within-city moves are made in search of improved housing conditions.

For those not living in poor housing in prairie inner cities, there are always emergency shelters and the street. According to the 1996 census, Winnipeg's Aboriginal population is approximately 50,000, the largest urban Aboriginal population in the country. The majority live in the inner city where they represent roughly a quarter of inner city residents. In addition to living in the worst housing (three-quarters have problems with housing conditions) and having the least income (of which half is spent on rent), they are also most likely to be subjected to discrimination by landlords. Given these statistics, it is not surprising that Winnipeg's Aboriginal population is well-represented among the homeless. A study of ten agencies that provide shelter and other services for the homeless found over half of those served were Native people. The Main Street Project alone, a crisis centre providing emergency shelter and drop-in for about 2,000 homeless a year, reported roughly 72 percent treaty and non-status Natives among its regulars.[1] Most were Ojibwa- or

Saulteaux-speaking, giving their original residence as reserves in south and central Ontario and Manitoba. Cree-speaking Natives (about 30 percent of the Aboriginal population served at the Main Street Project) came from northern Manitoba settlements.

Calgary has an Aboriginal population of approximately 24,000. The City of Calgary has conducted biennial surveys of agencies providing services to the homeless and found, in its 1998 survey, roughly 1,000 people using emergency shelters or living on the streets. All surveys throughout the 1990s showed that roughly 20 percent of the homeless in Calgary were Aboriginal. Edmonton's Aboriginal population is almost double that of Calgary and the proportion of Aboriginal people among the homeless is even more than double. On one night in 1999 the Edmonton Task Force on Homelessness counted over 800 homeless in shelters and on the street, of whom 42 percent, or 307, were Aboriginal. Two-thirds of Edmonton's homeless of all races were in shelters at the time of the count rather than on the street, while the opposite was true for Aboriginal people who were more likely to be on the street.

In Saskatchewan, the proportion of homeless Aboriginal people is even higher than in Alberta and Manitoba. There are roughly 15,000 Aboriginal people living in Regina where five emergency shelters and transition homes provide service to a total of roughly 80 homeless people each night. Almost 60 percent are Aboriginal, although they represent only seven percent of Regina's population. In Saskatoon 18,000 Aboriginal people live in the city, according to the 1996 census. And while this represents eight percent of Saskatoon's population, the four organizations providing emergency or transition beds report that almost 70 percent of shelter users are Aboriginal. Friendship Inn, a Saskatoon agency providing up to 300 meals a day, reports that 90 percent of those served are Aboriginal.

The homeless in Canada's prairie cities have not been squeezed out by gentrification. Poverty has simply shut them out of the housing market, even at its lowest end. In Winnipeg over half of those shut out are Aboriginal; in Regina and Saskatoon the proportion is roughly two-thirds. The Aboriginal homeless in Edmonton are not much better off (they make up 42 percent of Edmonton's homeless); in Calgary, where less than three percent of the city's population is Aboriginal, they represent 20 percent of the homeless.

Over 57 percent of lone parents live below the poverty line in Canada. The situation is even worse for lone parents under 25, those with young children, and those with less than high school education. In fact, the incomes of many poor lone parents are so far below the poverty line they cannot feed and shelter their children without emergency services. So-called emergency services like homeless shelters and food banks have actually become a regular part of the life of many lone parents for whom they provide long-term rather than short-term help. This has not been kept a secret. Statistics Canada reports annually on Canadian incomes and the disproportionate share of poverty borne by lone parents. The media, in turn, give good coverage to Statistics Canada findings. The number of lone-parent families in poverty, however, continues to grow, doubling over 20 years while Canada's population has increased by only 26 percent.

Since almost three-quarters of poor lone parents are on welfare or employment insurance, their poverty is a sad commentary on the adequacy of welfare and EI payments in Canada. The straightforward solution of higher benefits to provide lone parents and their children with sufficient food and a roof over their heads has had no public support among other Canadians who have decided, one assumes, that the problems of lone-parent families are not their problems. Yet two-parent families are increasingly at risk of ending up in the same boat. Thirty years ago 20 percent of Canadian marriages ended in divorce; by the 1990s the proportion had risen to almost 30 percent. And while many two-parent families enjoy two incomes, the sudden drop to one income after marriage breakdown can be devastating for the parent left with the responsibility of raising young children. Only 17 percent of single-parent mothers in Canada receive support payments. Most end up on welfare.

By the late 1990s these were some of the tragic facts about the poverty of lone parents in Canada.[2]

- Over 57 percent were living below the poverty line

- compared to 12 percent of two-parent families.
- Among younger single-parent mothers—those under 25 years of age—virtually all (93 percent) were living in poverty.
- The poverty rate for single-parent mothers with two young children was 80 percent compared to 13 percent for two-parent families with two young children.
- Of single-parent mothers who had not completed high school, a substantial majority (83 percent) were poor, although even among those who had completed high school or further education almost half were poor.
- Over 70 percent of poor single-parent mothers were on welfare or EI compared to 50 percent of poor two-parent families.
- The total average income of single-parent mothers on welfare in 1997 was $13,000 ($9,000 welfare, $3,000 child benefits, $1,000 earnings from part-time work).
- Difficulties in getting child care keeps many single parents from going back to school or going to work; both are steps that would help get them off welfare.
- Single-parent mothers are lone parents for an average of five years.
- A larger proportion of Aboriginal women in Canada are lone parents, roughly 15 percent compared to seven percent of non-Aboriginal women.

For lone parents, as for Aboriginal people, it is often a short step from trying to make ends meet to being forced out of housing arrangements, whether by rent hikes they cannot afford or evictions or a combination of both. In a growing number of cases across Canada female heads of families with nowhere else to go are appearing at emergency shelters with their children.

As far back as the 1970s women and children sought shelter in transition homes to escape situations of domestic violence. In effect, these were new single-parent families needing a special kind of security and help with re-establishment in more permanent accommodation on their own. For many years these were the women reported among Canada's homeless. They have been joined, however, by female single parents who are not escaping abusive situations but who nonetheless have a need for shelter for themselves and their children. Trying to serve their own target group with limited resources, most transition homes for battered women cannot provide space for others. Women from non-violent situations have had to turn to emergency homeless shelters which have increasingly been pressed into providing service not only to singles but to families.

Families headed by women have increased among the homeless in many Canadian cities. In 1998 the Toronto task force on homelessness found that 37 percent of adults using shelters were female heads of families, up from 24 percent only eight years earlier. The increase was caused by a rising number of poor households that were unable to afford available housing. These affordability problems were concentrated in the central area where a greater proportion of lone-parent households, particularly at the low end of the income scale, were located. The number of inner city lone-parent families with annual incomes under $20,000, for example, was double that in other regions of greater Toronto.

In Calgary the biennial survey of 1998 showed a 50 percent increase over 1994 in the number of homeless families in shelters. Most were headed by women. Over just four years the proportion of families headed by women and housed in women's shelters grew from half of all homeless families to three-quarters. An Edmonton task force study a year later found more than half of homeless families in Edmonton were single-parent families although they represented only 16 percent of families in the general population. Agencies serving the homeless in Edmonton reported increasing numbers of women on the street.

A 1996 Canada Mortgage and Housing study asked people working with the homeless across the country about the homelessness of women in particular.[3] In BC shelter workers reported more women using food banks and soup kitchens as a result of welfare cuts. Ontario workers also saw social assistance cuts as the cause of many women losing their housing and turning to Out of the Cold programs. In Quebec, where there are few shelter resources for homeless mothers and children, workers reported that the government will intervene and place the children in care if a mother loses her housing. Finding affordable housing is difficult for women in Saskatchewan, according to those who work with the homeless. It is especially difficult for Aboriginal women with children and the problem is made worse by the lack of shelter accommodation for women and their children in some urban areas. Alberta workers also pointed to a shortage of housing that women can afford as the reason for their growing numbers among the homeless in Edmonton and Calgary. Female lone parents who receive social assistance, they suggested, may also be victims of discrimination in their search for rental housing.

There were few comments by workers on how the children of lone-parent families coped with life in a homeless shelter. Many shelters, of course, do not remain open during the day. In New York City special buses pick up children at homeless shelters throughout the city and take them to various inner city schools. If this is the next step for Canadian homeless children, if this acceptance of a more or less permanent home for families in emergency shelters becomes part of the Canadian way of life, it may be time for us to listen.

While most Aboriginal people and most lone parents in Canada face poverty every day, the outlook is even more bleak for Aboriginal people who are also lone parents. Their plight is a growing problem, especially in urban areas in the West where they are heavily concentrated. Families headed by women make up the majority of all Aboriginal families in urban centres. With higher rates of migration than all other Aboriginal people (and all other Canadians), they bring to the city their native-ness and their lone-parent-ness and they set out to raise their young families with two strikes already against them. Three-quarters of urban Aboriginal lone parents are living far below the poverty line. Most live in substandard housing which they are constantly at risk of losing because of their inadequate incomes. As a result, Aboriginal lone parents are highly mobile within the city. Census data show that more than half move to improve their housing conditions. As in the case of lone-parent families in the general population (and to an even greater degree), Aboriginal lone-parent families are often one step away from eviction and ultimately homelessness.

Invisible in the political process, they can look in vain for any likelihood of change to their situation. By definition they are part of the Aboriginal peoples of Canada but they are generally not well-represented by Native organizations predominantly made up of men. As women, they are part of the larger society of Canadian women, but unfortunately Aboriginal lone parents are not on the agendas of mainstream women's interest groups. One analyst of urban Native policies has called them "the overlooked of the neglected,"[4] a fitting if not understated description of their place in the priorities of Canadians.

With a shortage of low-rent housing and an abundance of poor people, thousands of Canadians have become homeless since the early 1980s. While poverty waits to be addressed (and there is no evidence that we should hold our breath while waiting), the logical solution would appear to be subsidized housing. Unfortunately senior levels of government in Canada have pulled out of subsidized housing and there has been little protest. While local governments struggle with solutions on a limited tax base, more and more Canadians are left without shelter.

CHAPTER 7

Slums to Social Housing to Streets

The poor have always needed help with some of the basic necessities of life. Recognition of this reality came slowly to Canadians in the 20th century, but by the middle of the Depression years when unemployment spread into the middle class the average Canadian accepted the need for a public role in helping those who were down and out to survive. Emergency relief measures during the Depression were followed by more permanent legislation in the early years of World War II when unemployment insurance came into effect. Family allowance payments came near the end of the war, as did the beginnings of plans for broader social security programs. The government's role was seen as strengthening incomes which, in turn, would find their way (through spending) into an invigorated national economy at war's end.

Solutions to housing problems, however, were not so straightforward. In fact, strengthened personal incomes were intended to help Canadians afford housing that was often unaffordable. Despite the thousands of personal tragedies during the Depression, the public had not lost faith completely in the free market system. Concern for the poor was not extended to public provision of housing although rent payments took up a disproportionate amount of low incomes. This lack of concern was historically consistent. For 30 years following the end of World War I, government action on housing was sporadic and scattered. Its most significant feature was its failure to help the lowest-income group of Canadians but, in fairness, such help was never the intention of its policies.

❖   ❖   ❖   ❖   ❖   ❖

While governments at all levels experimented with a mixed bag of housing actions in the first half of the 20th century, the poor coped with housing problems in their own way with as much or as little success as any of the government programs. Early in the century on the edge of Canada's growing cities the lowest-paid workers created communities of shacks and cabins made of salvaged lumber and insulated only with cardboard. In 1908 the *Toronto Globe*, having set up a relief fund for the "shackers" on the outskirts of the city, thanked the public for its support after a week of the most severe weather recorded in a generation:

> Without the supplies so enthusiastically provided, the shackers would have suffered terribly... The fund is being spent on the relief of those living in shacks beyond the boundaries of the city, and for whom the city of Toronto has no responsibility. Not less than 1,500 of these people are depending for daily bread on the fund...

Settlements on the fringe of town were generally tolerated by municipal authorities because they provided a pool of labour for some of the least desirable jobs in an expanding manufacturing centre. World War I drained away many of the residents of shanty towns, as did boom times. Even when shanty towns were full, however, their dilapidated shacks were only temporary homes to many who drifted in and out of the city outskirts to other city outskirts in search of work.

But not all the poor lived in shanty towns. More permanent city residents at the low end of the wage scale were concentrated in slum areas within the city limits, areas characterized by overcrowding, deteriorating buildings, lack of sanitary facilities, and poor maintenance. Slums were usually located near railway tracks or industrial areas. A few slum dwellers owned their homes but the vast majority were tenants of slum landlords.

In good times and bad times the poor lived in shanty towns and slums in Canada's early industrial years. In the period leading up to World War I, however, low-wage workers in urban centres experienced significantly more severe housing problems ranging from shortages to inaccessibility due to high rents. Across the country rentals increased by 62 percent from 1900 to 1913 while wages increased by only 44 percent. (In Montreal and Toronto, in particular, rents doubled while wages rose by only 32 to 35 percent.) Part of the problem was supply. The economic slump of 1913 was especially hard on the construction industry. A sag in profits brought most house building to a halt, adding to shortages and contributing to the rent crisis.

In response to the housing crisis governments in Quebec, Nova Scotia, and Ontario brought in legislation for limited dividend housing, an arrangement that encouraged the construction of new houses by offering low-interest loans to builders who agreed to limit their profits to a ceiling set by the government. In those few attempts to solve the crisis across the country housing was seen as a provincial issue, and none of the three provinces asked for federal assistance. Rental units built by limited-dividend corporations alleviated a small portion of housing shortages, but the costs of building units that met acceptable housing standards put rents out of reach of the lowest-income families. This was a disappointing but not too troubling outcome, offset as it was by the boost given by government financial assistance to the sagging construction industry.

Government and private funds for limited-dividend construction were diverted during the war to other, more pressing needs. By 1918 there was little construction activity; housing shortages mounted and the industry again needed a shot in the arm. This time the provinces convinced the federal government that the crisis was war-related and logically warranted federal action. It came in the form of $25 million in loans for housing, low-interest loans to be made to provincial governments that, in turn, would lend to municipalities and ultimately to private builders. Limits were imposed on the costs of the new homes in order to reach the average workingman.

It was cost ceilings, however, that brought about the failure of the program. Municipalities complained that ceilings were unrealistically low for builders who were forced to cut corners, invariably producing unsound homes. In response to municipal complaints, ceilings crept up during the life of the program and, in the end, it benefitted only the top 20 percent income group of the population. Once again, the outcome failed to distress policy-makers. Government officials conceded that, besides the goal of alleviating housing shortages, the program had been aimed at creating employment in the construction industry and averting potential labour unrest at the end of the war. Ironically the one municipality where the federal loan program was viewed as a success by its proponents was Winnipeg whose low-interest loans were not particularly aimed at industrial workers but went, for the most part, to white-collar workers who already owned their own lots. As the Winnipeg General Strike unfolded over the next 12 months, few municipal or federal officials could claim the loan program had successfully averted labour unrest.

In the economic recovery of the 1920s the construction industry prospered and reached boom proportions. There were no demands for government intervention in housing. Despite better economic times, the poor continued to live in slums. Solutions were confined to demolition of substandard slum housing by public health officials (with no alternative provision for the displaced tenants) or exhorting the poor to pull themselves up by the bootstraps. The latter prescription was the one favoured by the emerging social work profession which blamed the plight of the poor on the poor themselves and which made it their mission to teach slum dwellers better management of their meager resources.

The Great Depression, however, brought new demands for government housing assistance. The construction industry had again collapsed after a prosperous decade, putting many out of work. By 1935 the federal government was looking at any and all proposals for the stimulation of industry and employment. The US had already implemented its New Deal policies, and the Canadian government was urged to do the same. Following pressure from the construction industry and municipalities across the country, Prime Minister Bennett agreed to include a federal housing program in his own New Deal.

Leading up to the legislation, many presentations to a parliamentary committee on housing proposed publicly subsidized low-rental housing as a solution. These public housing proposals were based on the concept of direct low-interest loans to municipalities that would provide public housing for low-income tenants. Bennett ignored his parliamentary committee's recommendations for rental housing and opted instead for a joint loan system in which the federal government contributed 20 percent of the cost of a new home if a private lending institution loaned the first 60 percent. Even the administration of the government 20 percent loan would be made through private lenders. Home ownership was the goal, and those who had to rent were left out of public plans for housing assistance. Though the government's plan, which became the Dominion Housing Act of 1935, was intended to accommodate private lending institutions in Canada by staying out of the mortgage market, it was the private lenders who finally scuttled the new housing program. Lending companies administering the program openly complained to applicants about federal terms and red tape and often talked them out of participating. More important, private lenders were inclined to regard many working-class communities as risky for mortgage lending, rejecting applications from those neighbourhoods and denying the benefits of the Housing Act to the very people who most needed help.

John Bacher, Canadian researcher and historian in the area of housing policy, quotes from the private correspondence of David Mansur, chief inspector of mortgages for the Sun Life Assurance Co. of Canada, who admitted that "practically the whole population earning less than $1,500 a year will be not considered for loans under the Act." (Significantly 80 percent of male Canadian workers in the early 1930s earned less than $1,450.) Instead, according to Mansur, the Dominion Housing Act benefitted only an affluent minority. But, in fact, the federal government had never claimed otherwise. The 1935 Act's three primary purposes had been to set housing standards, stimulate housing construction, and reduce the high rate of unemployment.

In all, during its three years of operation, only 3,000 joint loans were made under the Dominion Housing Act while surveys estimated 10,000 people with housing needs in Montreal alone, 1,300 in Winnipeg, 2,000 in Toronto, and 1,000 in Regina. A change in government brought in new legislation designed to fill the gaps in the old. The preamble to the new legislation, the National Housing Act of 1938, was an encouraging sign. It specified that the Act was intended to stimulate the construction of houses *for persons with a small income.* As such, it contained provision for direct loans of up to 90 percent to local housing authorities for low-rental housing. Sadly the public low-rental housing portion of the new legislation never produced a single unit of shelter across the country before it expired in 1940. Critics pointed to several reasons for the lack of take-up, all attributed to government reluctance to get into public housing in the first place, despite stating the opposite in the legislation. The government's mental block was related to the *public* part of public housing, where governments (federal, provincial, and municipal) bypassed the private marketplace for mortgages and made arrangements that were suspiciously socialistic or, at best, social democratic, both possibilities equally frightening in the late 1930s. Features of the new legislation that many felt were intended to discourage builders were cost ceilings set below actual costs necessary to build the units, taxation restrictions on participating municipalities (taxes could be no more than one percent of construction costs of the new housing), and the requirement that provincial governments guarantee the loans. Many provinces declined to pass the necessary legislation.

Although the federal government was reluctant to provide public housing during the late years of the Depression, it took on this role a few years later as an emergency wartime measure. Wartime Housing Ltd., a federal agency created early in the 1940s, constructed and managed low-rent units for munitions workers from 1941 to 1945, and it continued after the war with units for returning veterans right up until 1949. Wartime Housing provided rental accommodation; the program was not aimed at home ownership (as earlier federal programs had been) for the obvious reason of its temporary nature. A highly successful program, it was seen by many as the solution to peacetime housing problems, especially in light of the growing recognition that low-income Canadians would benefit more from rental rather than home ownership programs. Despite public pressure, however, Wartime Housing was wound down, and its high-level construction activity was not picked up in newly drafted legislation. Instead of 100 percent federally funded housing projects, which had produced over 40,000 Wartime Housing rental units from 1941 to 1949, a new formula of 75 percent federal funds and 25 percent provincial funds effectively reduced production to a total of 11,000 units over the next 15 years.

The impetus to public housing in peacetime finally came from federal offers to help municipalities clear out unsightly slums. By the mid-1950s the public housing situation in Canada was dramatically changed by new legislation that shared the cost of urban renewal with cities across the country. Urban renewal has been mentioned earlier (Chapter 3) in connection with the loss of low-income housing in Canada's major cities. It involved the clearing of slum areas and their replacement with low-rent public housing projects. Half the cost of slum clearance was borne by the federal government; 75 percent of new public housing was also federally funded. In addition, operating losses could also be shared, an arrangement that made it possible for provinces and municipalities to provide rental subsidies. The poor were now being considered in housing policies. It would be some time, however, before they realized their needs were secondary to the more exciting objective (for city administrations) of removing blighted areas and turning their urban pride-and-joys into centres to attract industry or tourists or new permanent residents or perhaps all three.

Urban renewal—including both its parts, slum clearance and public housing for former slum tenants—was heralded as an ideal solution for housing the poor. But no one, not one housing planner in Canada, the US, Britain, and some other European countries, predicted that urban renewal would give public housing such a bad name that it would be dropped unceremoniously from the public agendas of all those countries within a few years and would never recover. To note that there were unintended consequences to the urban renewal program is an understatement. Chronologically the first problem that arose was the failure to provide displaced slum tenants with new public housing units within any kind of acceptable time frame. In Halifax, for example, demolition in the Jacob Street area was undertaken in early 1958 while public housing was not completed until late 1960. Later in Hamilton, demolition of slums in 1965 was followed by completion of public housing as late as 1969. Placement in a public housing unit sometimes never took place at all. In Montreal almost 1,800 families were displaced by urban renewal while only 800 new public housing units were built. Federal legislation required that families dispossessed by clearance were to be offered accommodation in rentals "that in the opinion of the Minister and the municipality, are fair and reasonable, having regard to family incomes, etc." Many displaced residents, in fact, were left with higher housing costs after moving out.

When the new public housing projects were filled in the 1960s and early 1970s another problem surfaced. Despite the fact that earlier there had been a heavy concentration of the poor in slum areas, to everyone's distress there was a delayed recognition that now there was a heavy concentration of the poor in public housing projects. Ghettos were bad enough in the inner city, bringing together in a few acres a multitude of what were called "problem families." But many housing projects born of urban renewal were located at the periphery of city centres, and the concentration of poor families was not welcomed by their middle-class neighbours. Indeed in many cities the old city limits were as far as planners could go in locating public housing. Most suburban homeowners made it clear to their local councils that they did not want public housing projects in their backyards.

Problems with housing design also became apparent after millions had been spent. High-rise apartment blocks, although cost-effective in land use, were not suitable for families who needed instead ground-oriented units to accommodate their children's activities and supervision. In the absence of outdoor play areas, elevators, stairwells, and hallways became recreational space for children. One-room bachelorettes made depressing homes for seniors. They increased the sense of isolation and provided restricted living space for an age group more inclined to stay home than venture out every day, especially in winter. Housing design was also responsible for a host of privacy issues. Large numbers of housing units used a single entrance, a problem as common to a row of attached two-storey units as to high-rises. Undefined public open spaces in projects meant that many two-storey family units lacked even a minimal private area that could be called a yard. A further problem reinforced by design was a sense of segregation from the surrounding community. Units tended to face inwards onto a courtyard or other common space rather than facing the public street. In addition, streets into the projects were generally culs-de-sac, not through streets, emphasizing that the project was an entity in itself to planners, not a group of homes whose residents were part of the larger city.

The most outstanding issue, however, for project residents surveyed across the country was the quality of management. Getting normal repairs completed was never straightforward for tenants. They frequently had to make requests to a central bureaucracy where a tedious system of priorities left many waiting for periods that would never be tolerated in the private rental sector. There were also complaints that local superintendents were insensitive and tended to treat tenants as welfare clients, which said a lot about the perceived treatment of welfare clients. Long waiting lists for public housing were a disincentive to management taking any steps to respond to signs of tenant dissatisfaction.

All these problems arose with the public housing projects that followed the demolition of hundreds of acres of urban slums across the country. But the demolition itself came under attack as the bulldozer approach often removed much housing stock that was not substandard, including many historic pieces of property that would have added a certain amount of character to neighbourhoods if they had escaped the mass destruction. In some communities—in Halifax, Montreal, Toronto, Hamilton, and Vancouver— neighbourhood struggles successfully halted part of the destruction by the late 1960s, but for many it was too late.

Most of the problems associated with public housing in the 1960s had obvious solutions that could have been implemented while still maintaining a public housing program. But when they were brought to light publicly by the Hellyer Task Force on Housing and Urban Development (1969), the result was the termination of new public housing construction funded by the federal government and the introduction of policies that would emphasize housing the poor in ways that would not stigmatize them. Rather than ghettos of low-income residents, smaller-scale projects that housed residents with a range of incomes were to receive federal funding in the form of 100 percent mortgage assistance. These mixed-income projects were provided by non-profit or cooperative housing corporations which assigned a quarter of the project units to low-income tenants in exchange for the 100 percent loans. The federal government subsidized the rents of low-income tenants and, in effect, subsidized the rents of all income groups in these projects by paying the difference between what tenants paid and actual costs. Not only were projects smaller and better designed to accommodate their predominantly middle-class residents, but mixed-income housing also got around the problem of neighbourhood resistance. With these advantages, cooperative housing proved very popular during the 1970s. Actively promoted by Canada Mortgage and Housing, cooperative units grew from 1,500 in 1973 to 22,000 in 1978, almost all located in Ontario, Quebec, Manitoba, and British Columbia. Only a quarter to a third of these, however, were for low-income tenants.

By the 1980s federal enthusiasm for non-profit and cooperative housing had waned. Times had changed. Economic restraint and a concern for federal budget deficits brought in policies aimed at reducing public-sector spending. The government began to shift responsibility for social housing to the provincial level, partly for reasons of appropriate jurisdiction and partly to involve the provinces in subsidizing their own social housing residents. The goal was to download both administration and subsidies. What had worked in the 1970s was now receiving some second thoughts; the popularity of mixed-income housing projects had come at high cost. First, there was the burden of rent subsidies to the low-income quarter of all residents—the poor who earlier had been the target of public housing. These residents were the most heavily subsidized, the subsidy equal to the difference between their incomes and actual costs (mortgage payments and operating costs). But second, and growing each year, was the burden of subsidizing the rents of non-poor residents in mixed-income projects, a group allowed to pay rents comparable to rents in the low end of the private market even though they were considerably lower than actual costs. These non-poor residents were actually receiving a shallow subsidy and, since they represented three-quarters of all mixed-income project residents, the cost of their subsidies became the larger portion of the total cost. And, with skyrocketing interest rates in the early 1980s, the total cost was causing alarm at the federal level.

Against this background of rising social housing costs and federal downloading to the provinces, the government announced in 1985 that federal assistance in the future would be available only to low-income households. In mixed-income projects residents of moderate and upper income would no longer be subsidized.[1] For their part, the provinces began to drop non-poor residents from non-profit housing, reducing the income mix which had been championed a decade earlier. By the late 1980s the federal government began to cut back on new commitments to cost-share social housing, even for the newly targeted low-income residents. From over 20,000 units cost-shared in 1987, the number fell to less than 7,000 units by 1993 when total funding was frozen. The following year the government announced that new non-profit or cooperative units would no longer receive federal support. Ontario continued to fund new social housing without federal assistance, but most provinces cut back on housing expenditures. Finally in 1995 Ontario also closed the door on new social housing.

Prior to the 1950s Canadian housing policies were aimed at stimulating the economy by helping the construction industry build more houses and create more jobs. Even as it intervened to this extent the federal government pulled itself out of the direct lending business as soon as it could following the Depression and World War II and left the mortgage market to private lenders (with federal government guarantees). Housing the poor was never the goal— policy-makers held fast to the economic theory that building new housing for upper-income households would create a supply of houses for the middle-income group as upper-income families left their homes and moved into new and better housing. In turn, middle-income families would be leaving houses that would come within the budgets of the poor, a process of filtering that satisfied the economists and the policy-makers that the needs of low-income families would be taken care of in a free housing market. Some filtering did indeed take place but never down to the lowest income level with the result that poor households were more likely to be renters than homeowners.

Despite a history of policies aimed at home ownership, the federal government became involved with housing for low-income renters in the late 1950s and 1960s and, even then, its involvement was part of a larger plan to create employment by clearing out slums and building a better standard of housing. Nonetheless the poor benefitted with rents artificially geared to their incomes and with federal and provincial governments making up the shortfall. Canada was no better or worse than the US and Britain in the mistakes made in urban renewal. Disrupting old neighbourhoods and moving those who were displaced into new projects that turned out to be flawed in their design were problems for the poor. Creating ghettos and threatening property values in adjacent neighbourhoods were problems for the middle class. By the 1970s the federal government wanted out.

Mixed-income housing became the new solution. It avoided the problem of heavy concentrations of the poor in large projects. Moreover, the inclusion of middle-income tenants in mixed-income housing resulted in better housing design which competed favourably with middle-class homes in the same neighbourhoods. It was true that these new projects provided only a quarter of their units for low-income tenants but, given middle-class resistance to the old public housing approach, it was a trade-off the poor would have to accept. It was a quarter or nothing once public housing fell into disrepute.

Unfortunately the mixed-income solution of the 1970s had its critics. The very thing that made it palatable to nearby property owners—the predominance of middle-income tenants in mixed-income housing—was offensive to an increasing number of local taxpayers who saw their taxes being spent on subsidies to tenants whose incomes could quite readily allow them to rent in the private-sector rental market. With economic restraint in the 1980s the voices of mixed-income housing critics became louder. Governments at all levels responded with new policies that targeted tighter funding at low-income people, not only in the social housing area but in all social policy areas. Universal programs that reached non-poor Canadians, like family allowances and old age security, were subjected to heavy scrutiny. Mixed-income housing was simply another victim.

A review of government housing policies over the years is not complete without some basic arithmetic that demonstrates the contribution these policies have made to homelessness in the 1980s and 1990s. Slum clearance in the 1960s resulted in a net loss of low-income housing units in Canada (even after new public housing was in place), a loss readily conceded by the federal minister responsible for housing. By the 1970s new public housing which might have finally filled the gap was halted. In its place came mixed-income housing with only a quarter of units allocated to the poor. In other words, new housing for the poor was reduced by 75 percent which set it back even further from any possibility of ever regaining the existing net loss. Finally, with an increasing trend toward less generous attitudes on the part of Canadian taxpayers, all new social housing stopped without a murmur of protest. The final 25 percent was cut to zero. Add to this never-recovered loss the loss of inner city housing caused by gentrification which reduced the size of inner city populations by a total of over 250,000 in major cities across Canada and we have a recipe for a homeless crisis that grows with each year of public inaction.

CHAPTER 8

The Private-Sector Alternative

In its 60-year history of providing housing assistance the federal government could never make home ownership work for the poor. Down payments were increasingly reduced for government-guaranteed mortgages, but they still remained out of reach for workers whose incomes barely provided for the basic necessities of life and certainly left no room for savings. In addition, despite federal guarantees, private lenders had their own rules about eligible income levels for mortgages—after all, they had been in the business of measuring risks long before the government entered the field. And it was not only incomes. Sometimes entire neighbourhoods were ineligible, or red-lined, by lenders with concerns that property values in such low-income areas would not hold up (might even, in fact, fall below the value of the mortgage loan). Often it was simply that builders could not produce an acceptable quality of housing for a price the poor could afford.

These were obvious barriers to low-income home ownership. By 1970 only six percent of loans under the federal National Housing Act went to families in the bottom 40 percent income range, while 85 percent went to families in the next highest 40 percent. Still federal policy statements continued to declare (and federal governments continued to insist) that low-income households were indeed a target group. If loans were going only to middle-income housing, it was argued, the poor would benefit through filtering, described earlier in Chapter 7, a natural market phenomenon that had many adherents among economists through the years but little evidence of coming close to reality.

The truth was that low-income Canadians had to rent, not own. Policy-makers implicitly recognized this fact with the introduction of public rental housing in the 1960s, though the goal of home ownership for most Canadians was never abandoned. Besides direct government involvement in rental housing, federal policies before 1970 also made it attractive for the private sector to be active in the rental market by offering incentives to investment in residential rental property. On the tax side, a capital cost allowance of five percent treated depreciation somewhat generously compared to the allowance for other kinds of residential investment. There was also no tax on capital gains, and for many owners of rental property capital gains made up a larger portion of investment return than rental income. In addition, prior to 1971, investment on real estate could be used as a tax shelter by allowing losses to be applied against other income. On the financing side, federal loan insurance under the National Housing Act and direct lending by Canada Mortgage and Housing made new construction of rental housing attractive to builders. As a result of these incentives, the private rental market, even at the low end, was healthy as Canada's major cities experienced rapid growth.

Thirty years later the situation has dramatically changed. The federal government has stopped funding new construction of social housing (ending new public housing in the 1970s and cooperative or non-profit housing in the early 1990s). And while Canadians might logically look to the private sector to fill the gap, especially with a strong demand for low-income rental accommodation, there are many reasons why this is unlikely to happen. Construction of rental housing, in fact, has been all but abandoned by the private building industry over the past 15 years. New construction of rental apartments amounted to approximately 30,000 units in 1986. In 1999 only 7,000 new rental units were built in all urban centres across the country.[1] By way of comparison, during the same period annual condominium starts increased by 10,000 units, with over 24,000 condos being built in 1999.

Rental housing lost its attractiveness for the private building industry for many reasons. As far back as 1971 some of the earlier incentives were dropped by the federal government. Capital gains tax was introduced on all financial and real estate investment except a principal residence. Not only was the investor faced with a capital gains tax on resale, new limits were placed on the postponing of recaptured depreciation. These two changes effectively lowered the liquidity of rental property and eliminated a whole range of investors whose primary objective was profits made on resale. The same 1971 tax revisions also cut back on the use of real estate as a tax shelter by allowing only companies in the business of real estate to apply losses to other income.

By the mid-1970s there were further disincentives to the construction of rental housing. With the introduction of wage and price controls at the federal level as an anti-inflation measure, almost all provincial governments brought in rent controls (rent control had been in place in Quebec since the early post-war period). These measures, probably more than any other, discouraged new rental construction. In the absence of an open market, potential rents were held in check and investors were faced with lower returns from rental income.

In addition to lowering rental income, rent controls had the potential to lower the capital value of rental property, creating another deterrent to investment. Owners generally had two or three options: absorb rental income losses and simply make less money, cut back on maintenance and repairs in order to offset rental income losses, or sell the property by converting the units to condominiums. For many who chose the second option, rental properties with reduced maintenance soon deteriorated and their capital value decreased. If owners could find any buyers in the no-longer-attractive rental housing market, their resale gains were therefore lowered even before capital gains tax was applied. With this door almost closed, a popular method of cutting losses was to convert to condominiums. Unfortunately for rental property owners, conversions were prohibited in several major cities, among them Toronto and Vancouver, even before rent controls were introduced. Provincial legislation later prohibited conversion in a wider range of municipalities.

Although the original intention in 1975 was to introduce rent controls for only a temporary period, only a few provinces had removed them by the 1980s and most are still in effect today. Once rent controls are in place there is no simple way to de-control, given a wide range of political pressures. The fact that a temporary measure became permanent because of the fear of political consequences has had yet another impact on the supply of private rental housing. Investors have never been fully confident that governments under pressure will not tighten controls further. Most provinces have exempted new rental housing from control, but "new" has been redefined in some cases over a period of time. Such legislative changes in the past have created uncertainty about future changes and have tended to make investors cautious about constructing new rental housing. An attempt at restoring confidence has been made in Ontario where the highly regulated rent control system in place since 1975 was recently relaxed.

Federal tax reform in the late 1980s brought another round of disincentives to private rental construction. The old manufacturers' tax on building materials was replaced by the Goods and Services Tax (GST) but the change also affected costs formerly not subject to tax. Since these new items made up a substantial portion of construction costs, the GST increased the total cost of rental construction for private builders. There have been varying estimates of the extent of the increase, ranging from three to five percent of the construction costs of an average unit. And while owner-occupied housing was eligible for a rebate of 2.5 percent in recognition of GST-induced increases to purchase prices, rental housing missed out on such a break for almost a decade.[2]

Increased construction costs due to the GST lowered the rates of return for investors in rental property, a decrease which translated into reduced property values. The Canadian Tax Foundation estimated the decrease in these asset values at three percent. Earlier disincentives had started new rental construction on its downward plunge; now there was even more reason to avoid this area of the housing market. (The same tax reform package also reduced the capital cost allowance and increased the capital gains tax.) In the years immediately following the introduction of the GST, rental construction showed its most dramatic decline. Construction of private rental units in Vancouver fell from approximately 1,150 to 470 annually in a four-year period, a decrease of almost 60 percent.[3] Calgary's rental housing drop was 82 percent between 1992 and 1996, a year when only 15 new rental units were built in the city.

And while rental units dropped by 82 percent, Calgary condo units went up by 80 percent. Toronto was also affected, showing a reduction of over 500 annual rental starts between 1992 and 1994. In 1994 only 57 private rental units were built in the greater Toronto area.

Tax changes have been costly for the building industry, especially for those investing in rental properties. But increased government regulation has added another burden and another reason for builders to choose other sectors of the industry. The decline in new rental construction starts has to be attributed in part to the increasing costs of building code changes. National building standards go as far back as World War II when wartime housing was directly undertaken by the federal government. Standards were laid down in a National Building Code. The code went on to become the basis for building and apartment standards used by Canada Mortgage and Housing in making NHA loans following the war. In addition to ensuring the long-term value of NHA-financed homes, the National Building Code was intended to maintain public health and safety. Over the next two decades national standards were made more flexible to reflect new housing forms and tenure arrangements, new lot sizes to accommodate more affordable housing, and the unique requirements of different regions of the country. Finally, in light of the growing number of regulations imposed by other levels of government, the federal government dropped the requirement for national standards for all insured lending in 1980.

Since 1980 it has not been national standards so much as provincial and local building standards that have increased construction costs. Requirements vary among jurisdictions with the result that building code changes present a greater problem in some areas of the country than others. A survey conducted by the Canadian Home Builders' Association found that a substantial 45 percent of builders in Manitoba and Saskatchewan considered more onerous building code requirements a critical problem. Just as many claimed that problems related to *municipal* approvals and standards were also critical. A third of builders in BC reported problems with provincial building code requirements and only slightly less with municipal approvals and standards. The same percentage in the Atlantic region reported problems with the municipal approval process. While not identifying provincial code requirements as a major problem, well over a third of builders in Alberta expressed concern about potential municipal requirements for sprinkler systems.

In Ontario the president of Ottawa's largest private residential builder and landlord, Minto Developments, claimed that amendments to the Ontario Building Code in the 1990s added substantially to the cost of housing, increasing construction costs by as much as $8,000 per home. In the case of rental construction, almost $70 per month per unit was added to costs (and was clearly not recoverable in the level of rents the market would allow). The Minto president added:

> Additional changes to building and fire codes have increased the cost of housing through regulations that set unnecessarily high standards. No one can deny that the housing being built today is better than what was built 10 years ago. However, Minto currently provides good quality housing to approximately 10,000 families in Ottawa-Carleton in accommodations that were built years before these amendments came into place. The residents who are living in these homes continue to indicate their satisfaction with the housing and its cost. In light of this response, we must ask a fundamental question: are our housing standards becoming too high?[4]

Increased government regulation at the provincial level also includes new measures to protect consumers, regulations that have been introduced in Quebec and BC with added costs for builders. In Quebec a provincial regulatory body is responsible for the inspection of building sites to verify that each worker at the site has a "competency" card. This is part of a mandatory plan under which certificates of competence are required for all construction personnel. Consumers are also protected by a guarantee against building defects not corrected satisfactorily by contractors. Another government agency collects fees from contractors for mandatory building licenses which can be rescinded if the contractor employs a worker without a competency certificate and for a variety of other reasons. (To obtain these certificates workers must become members of one of five unions designated by the Quebec government.) Each of these requirements for certificates, licenses, and guarantees adds to the builders' costs, including higher labour costs. Builders of both ownership and rental housing for resale are affected. For investors in rental property the costs must be added to GST and building code costs for a sector of the building industry already on the decline.

Guarantees for consumers have also increased building costs in BC. A new Home Owners Protection Act requires builder licensing and mandatory third-party warranty, both requirements resulting from problems in the 1990s with building defects that plagued condo owners in the greater Vancouver area. A substantial portion of the new cost to builders is a contribution of $750 per unit to a reconstruction fund to cover provincial loans to owners of the affected condos. With the introduction of mandatory guarantee programs in both Quebec and BC, there are indications that the building industry may be facing a whole new set of costs as it conducts business in the 21st century.

Municipal governments have also contributed to the growing number of regulations and levies affecting the building industry. In recent years development charges imposed by municipalities have added significant costs to new housing developments. These charges, to cover the cost of infrastructure for new housing (major items like the construction of roads, sewers, and other capital projects), have grown as senior levels of government have increasingly left the burden on municipalities. Many municipalities, in turn, have chosen not to finance infrastructure from general revenues but instead have passed the costs on to builders and ultimately to buyers. In the late 1980s development charges expanded in some provinces to include the costs of other services (education, parks, and schools, for example) which were judged to be necessary for the population growth arising from new development. Since the inclusion of these new growth-related costs, development charges in some areas of the country have tripled or quadrupled their previous levels.

Rental housing construction has been hit hard by development charges. Estimates of cost have ranged from $8,000 to $17,000 *per rental unit* compared to a typical development charge (or lot levy) that ran around $5,000 before federal and provincial governments withdrew considerable funding. When builders across the country were surveyed by the Canadian Home Builders' Association in 1999, 44 percent of Manitoba and Saskatchewan builders, and a quarter to a third of builders in Ontario and BC, considered development charges a critical problem. By 2000 the federal government committed new funds to a municipal infrastructure program intended to help with the growing burden of development charges imposed by municipalities.

Investors in private residential rental properties complained about tax treatment by some municipalities in Canada long before development charges shot upward. In collecting local property taxes, these municipalities usually taxed apartment rental properties at a higher rate than single-family homes and often taxed them higher than commercial properties. In fact, this differential tax treatment was as much a responsibility of provincial governments as it was of local governments. Recent legislation in Ontario has attempted to make the property tax system fairer by allowing developers of new rental projects to avoid the higher taxes by registering them as condominiums. Prior to this change, the difference between residential categories was applied at the assessment level where properties are assessed at a ratio of market value. In large urban areas like East York, apartment buildings could be assessed at as much as four-and-a-half times the assessment rate of single homes. In smaller municipalities like Fort Erie or St. Catharines apartment buildings could be assessed at twice the rate. In other provinces, Alberta and Manitoba, for example, the difference has been applied at the mill rate level and has been called a split mill rate. In Calgary, before recent changes, property tax mill rates for apartment buildings could be one-and-a-third times the rate for single-family homes.

A Canadian Tax Foundation analysis points out that the differential tax treatment for multiple-unit rental property has never been defended by either provincial or municipal governments on the grounds of different or higher costs in providing services to these properties.[5] Instead the fact that differential treatment exists reflects how easy it is, relatively, to impose higher tax rates on certain categories of property. Owners of single-family homes tend to be more vocal about unfair taxes than tenants who are generally unaware of the tax on their apartments. In other words, it is easier politically to tax rental properties than it is to tax owner-occupied properties.

Owners of private-sector rental housing are landlords as well as investors. The potential investor's role as a landlord has tended to be less attractive as landlord/tenant legislation has shifted in favour of tenants' rights vis-à-vis landlords' rights. Across the country the security of tenure has been greatly increased for tenants over the past 20 to 30 years by provincial legislation introduced to redress former imbalances. It is fair to say that landlords, especially landlords of low-income tenants who took advantage of tenants' poor bargaining power in the past by refusing to make repairs or by evicting without cause, have justifiably been forced to comply with certain obligations. But compliance has not been attained without cost. Even when the cause of lease termination is persistent failure to pay rent, the landlord is faced with longer periods of notice, costly time spent in court proceedings, and statutory delays in recovering arrears deposited with the court. When the cause of termination is undue damage to premises (one of only six causes allowed under most legislation), the landlord no longer has recourse to recovering costs by a security deposit.

In his extensive review of landlord and tenant legislation in Ontario, Donald Lamont has acknowledged that residential tenants had little bargaining power in the years before legislation. The 1969 Landlord and Tenant Act achieved fairer balancing of the respective rights and obligations of landlords and tenants. Subsequent tighter amendments were aimed at the same objective. This would appear to be the case in most provinces. "However," Lamont comments, "one may wonder whether perhaps the pendulum has swung too far in favour of tenants."[6] On many occasions landlords have been required to take undue lengths of time and incur substantial legal costs in order to terminate leases that have clearly been violated.

Tightened landlord/tenant regulations can also make landlords more wary about taking tenants they consider higher risks. A recent Canada Mortgage and Housing study found landlords souring on rental investment in general, more than half expressing the opinion that the rental environment was worse than it had been five to ten years earlier.[7] In discussing tenants specifically, a majority of landlords agreed that the proportion of tenants they would consider high risk or undesirable was increasing. Researchers attributed this increase to the fact that over the period many Canadian renters with better income prospects had become homeowners, leaving landlords with a lower-income group as potential tenants. In support of this argument, income statistics showed that over the past two decades the average (real) income of the total group of renters in Canada declined by seven percent. And with this new profile of tenants in the private rental sector, landlords in their investor role had another reason to become less interested in rental investment. They were not so much personally prejudiced against low-income applicants as simply associating them, especially those at the lowest income level like welfare recipients and lone parents, with risk of default and bad debt.

Leaving aside non-tax changes like landlord/tenant legislation and rent controls that have pushed up costs for rental investors in recent years, the abandonment of new rental construction in Canada is very much in the nature of a taxpayers' revolt. Certainly it qualifies as a strike. When federal and provincial governments withdrew from social housing in the early 1990s their actions were frequently justified by the benefits of returning the rental construction field to private industry (which had clearly forsaken it). Ontario Housing Minister Al Leach promised, when funding for non-profit housing was stopped, that the province's housing needs would be met more efficiently by getting the private sector back into the business of building rental units.

Policies at all three levels of government, however, have done little to encourage the private sector. Even as the building industry's lobby organization, the Canadian Home Builders' Association, presses governments to reduce over regulation and taxes, it has made no promises about the private sector's ability to produce affordable housing for low-income tenants in a market completely free of government intervention. It favours instead the concept of shelter allowances which make direct payments to tenants and leave the building industry to produce housing units with a guarantee that costs will be covered. Shelter allowances are currently provided in

Canada as a component of social assistance delivered by provincial governments. They are also provided to seniors in some provinces— BC, Manitoba, Quebec, and New Brunswick. Proposals to solve the housing problems of low-income people with shelter allowances would transfer their housing costs to the social assistance system where presumably those needing housing assistance would apply only for a shelter allowance. Out in the private market the two levels of shelter assistance would be consistent. There is a certain amount of merit in linking the two. Housing policy specifically for low-income Canadians would become social policy and most practitioners in the social policy field prefer (philosophically) to provide assistance to those in need by giving cash rather than in-kind services. Cash assistance in the form of shelter allowances would allow recipients the dignity of making their own choices in the market (as they do with food and other necessities) and setting their own spending priorities within their total income.

Several disadvantages to shelter allowances need to be considered as well. They would add no new rental construction to the housing stock. Not only has rental construction declined but it is worth recalling that Canada's inner cities have experienced a substantial loss of low-income housing through gentrification over the past 20 years. In addition, the shrinking rental market still contains a good deal of housing stock of poor quality, a problem that would not be addressed by shelter allowances. Indeed to the extent that allowances increase the number of low-income renters who can afford the lowest rents landlords have less incentive to improve the quality of their premises.

Finally, as will be shown in the following chapter, shelter allowances as "social policy" would operate within the same public opinion environment as all other social programs. Since the 1980s it has not been a generous environment, not even a friendly environment. Canadians have developed tougher attitudes toward the less fortunate, and their lack of compassion stands in the way of solutions that involve more transfer payments. Health and education with benefits for all income groups in Canada are finding their way back onto the public agenda, but new spending for social assistance with benefits only for the poor has failed to gain any popular support.

CHAPTER 9

Homeless in a Harsher Canada

Because their poverty exists in a relatively affluent society homeless people represent a social problem to be addressed by creative social policies. They are one more disadvantaged group. Because the poverty of the homeless, however, leaves them without shelter while the rest of us are well-housed, their problems are more likely to be addressed by housing policies. It is not surprising that the outcome has been less than successful. Housing policies have been primarily aimed at other objectives; stimulating the economy, creating employment, clearing out slums, and promoting home ownership are a few.

When governments at all levels became involved with public housing in the 1960s housing and social policies came together, but it was a brief liaison and those responsible for housing policy moved quickly back where they belonged, although not as quickly nor as completely as they would have liked. With the final demise of social housing in the 1990s the housing problems of low-income Canadians, especially the homeless, became exclusively a social problem.

In the past ten or 15 years, as many other unfortunate Canadians will attest, the last place any disadvantaged person wanted to be was in a group served by a Canadian social program. During that period the cutting back of employment insurance (EI) and social assistance programs, in particular, took place with the almost enthusiastic approval of the general public. Indeed the public led and the government followed as unemployed people across the country had their allowances cut and their honesty questioned by an increasingly tough Canadian public. If the homeless had any choice, they would surely not choose to be a social policy issue during the late 20th and early 21st century.

Tough public attitudes toward the poor were not always the case in Canada. A whole range of social programs was legislated during the postwar period and no historian has suggested they were crammed down the throats of the Canadian public. In 1950, some seven years before the federal government introduced hospital insurance, 80 percent of Canadians favoured such a plan, according to a Gallup poll. Old Age Security, introduced in 1951, was supported by two-thirds of those polled across the country. In the 1960s over 80 percent believed a proposed medicare plan would work. While these were responses to specific programs, more general feelings of compassion and tolerance were also in the hearts of Canadians. Asked about the causes of poverty, respondents to a poll were of the opinion that circumstances beyond the control of the poor were more often to blame for their plight than lack of effort. Even when asked if labour unions had been a good or bad thing for Canada, almost 70 percent of Canadians in 1950 felt they had been a good thing. In the 1960s over half of Canadians thought medicare should provide the same level of care for everyone, whether they were rich or poor. These are not the answers one would get today.

In the early 1970s there was still evidence of Canadians caring for each other. Almost 70 percent thought the government was doing too little for low-income citizens. There was even talk of a guaranteed annual income for all, a solution approved by 58 percent of those interviewed in a Gallup poll. When did Canadians lose that compassion? Economic restraint beginning in the mid-1970s started them down the slope, but the descent was slow at first. Restraint meant that priorities had to be set. Slowly and steadily the public gave less and less priority to the unfortunate. Specifically, programs endorsed during the war and post-war period began to be cut back or were under threat. Only a few years earlier unemployment insurance coverage had been expanded, reaching almost all categories of workers in Canada, the qualifying period was shortened, and benefits were increased. Polled across the country, the majority of Canadians approved of these changes. By 1975 when the unemployment rate had risen to 7.1 percent (up from 4.2 percent in the late 1960s) these earlier changes were suddenly considered too generous. The federal government began to cut back, supported by the results of public opinion polls.[1] In outlining the excessive demands on the UI fund in the preceding four years, Finance Minister John Turner made a point of tying the increases to overly generous UI provisions in 1971 rather than to the first setback to steady economic growth since the end of World War II. The 1971 changes had been so generous, he told the House of Commons, they had been responsible for "undesirable effects on work incentives." In fact, polls were now showing that almost 70 percent of Canadians felt the government was not strict enough in checking UI applicants and a surprising 85 percent believed there was a significant number of Canadians who used the UI plan "simply as a means of getting a paid vacation." This response was from the same cross-section of Canadians who had supported the more generous benefits of only four years earlier.

By the late 1970s unemployment had risen to almost nine percent. Despite the worldwide economic crisis Canadians began to read that the problem was with workers themselves. It was suggested by opinion leaders that many held on to their jobs only for the number of weeks required to qualify for UI benefits. Presumably they would not bother to work at all if it were not for those mandatory qualifying weeks. Surprisingly this assessment of the situation was never seriously challenged by the public even though most were of labour force age. The assessment, in fact, seemed to hit a responsive chord. There was little protest when the qualifying period was extended from 8 to 12 weeks which, the government claimed, would give many workers an incentive to work longer. Since there had been little challenge to the original premise, who could argue with the conclusion that four more weeks added to the qualifying period would translate into four more weeks of work (and reduce the claims on the already strapped UI fund)? A year later the qualifying period was extended still further (to 20 weeks for new entrants to the workforce) and benefits were reduced. Again the extension was attributed to the need to encourage workers to establish "longer attachments to the active workforce." These changes were accepted by a public now starting to believe that high unemployment was caused by the unemployed.

While these new beliefs were catching on, the Unemployment Insurance Commission announced in February of 1977 that its officials were clamping down on cheaters. The government's own figures showed that overpayments to UI applicants amounted to only 1.86 percent of the total benefits paid out. Still, a press release promised, "the Commission is pressing forward with programs to uncover fraud." The statements of public service officials reflected the government's new hard line and the public's growing acceptance that malingering was a national problem. One assistant deputy minister assured the *Toronto Star* that the 50,000 people who would be cut off UI by longer qualifying periods were "mostly young people, moving in and out of the labour force and using unemployment insurance to fatten their income." In any case, according to the assistant deputy minister, there would be new training programs for those who were lucky enough to receive benefits, and having UI recipients take part in training would assuredly be "better than having them lying in bed drinking beer." The public was left to wonder, in light of such damaging statements made in public, what officials were saying in private. The true story about Canadian workers had to be even worse.

More steps were taken over the next decade to detect abuse of unemployment insurance. The Employment and Immigration Department was soon able to make better checks on claimants who failed to report work and earnings with a new Report on Hirings system that gathered hiring information from employers. The publicity surrounding its introduction not only made UI claimants more honest; it helped convince the public that the less than two percent who failed to report their earnings were understated. A computerized post-audit program was also introduced with the intention of tracking down discrepancies in employment information given on UI claims. The department also undertook spot investigations for the purpose of detecting fraud. One after another the announcements of investigative procedures were made to a receptive public.

Unfortunately none of these measures attacked the real cause of high unemployment and demands on UI. By the end of the 1980s the unemployment rate was 9.5 percent. The worldwide economic recession had not yet turned around. Still the government responded to public misgivings about the motivation of the workforce by extending UI qualifying periods again. In addition, Employment and Immigration Minister Barbara McDougall announced in the House, penalties would be strengthened for "fraudulent use of the unemployment insurance program." In the last decade of the century the preoccupation with fraud reached dizzying heights. By 1992 unemployment had reached 11.3 percent. The UI rolls continued to increase which did not say much for the government's efforts of 15 years to lower the numbers by concentrating on fraud. Even if the one to two percent of dishonest claimants had been weeded out, a considerable amount of time and money had been spent in appeasing an angry public. And very little was done to point out that all these efforts were misdirected.

In fact, although UI overpayments had dropped slightly in recent years (and were now down to 1.3 percent of total benefits paid), officials claimed the decrease did not necessarily mean there was less abuse. Canadians could rest assured the Employment and Immigration Department would stay on the trail of cheaters. This was good news to those who were lucky enough to have jobs and who were not convinced that those without jobs deserved much sympathy. An Environics public attitude poll showed a fairly strong belief among Canadians that cheating by social program recipients was widespread. The compassion of the earlier part of the century had given way to suspicion and distrust. The pride in social programs that reflected Canada's collective approach to solving problems of financial need had given way to calls for less help and less generosity. The UI cuts would be the first of many. Deputy Prime Minister Don Mazankowski, sensitive to the new mood of the public, told the *Toronto Star* the government would not pander to "bleeding hearts" by spending more and more on social programs.

There were still more UI cuts in the 1990s and still more polling to take the temperature of the public. By reducing the benefits of "frequent users" of the system, a new change affected seasonal workers in Canada, many of whom lived in the Atlantic provinces. During the decision-making process, while a House of Commons committee conducted hearings across the country, the government's polls showed that three-quarters of Canadians favoured the reductions. In light of these findings, a two-tiered system was introduced under which seasonal workers were paid at a lower rate than others. Once the new regulation was in place the public was polled again with the same percentage of Canadians in support. A rather remarkable endorsement of the reliability of opinion polls, the results confirmed for the government that it had nothing to fear at election time by pursuing similarly tough policies in other areas. And even though over two-thirds of Canadians who were polled believed the new UI changes failed to address the real issue, which was job creation, the reason most frequently given for supporting tougher legislation was that it would stop abuse of the system.

After 50 years of unemployment insurance in Canada there was little concern that a national program (rather than nine provincial programs) had originally been introduced to balance out regional job market variations across the country, among other things. In the 1990s Canadians forgot the insurance principle that the premiums of rare claimants would help to pay the cost of frequent claimants. Instead the idea of evening out risks was rejected. Human Resources Minister Lloyd Axworthy explained why the frequent-user policy was being adopted: "People are saying, Why should one part of the country pay for another part of the country? Why should one industry pay for others?" It was clear Canadians across the country were starting to lose interest in looking out for each other. When the new UI regulation reducing benefits to seasonal workers was evaluated a few years later, it was found that it reduced 21 percent of claims in Canada as a whole, but it reduced 51 percent of claims in Prince Edward Island, 48 percent in Newfoundland, and 43 percent in New Brunswick.

People on welfare were next in line for the public's mistrust. There was, of course, a certain amount of logic and consistency in this development. Increasingly the jobless ended up on welfare as UI benefits ran out under stricter regulations. In 1989 roughly 74 percent of those officially unemployed were covered by unemployment insurance. This proportion dropped to 58 percent in 1992 and to 36 percent by the end of the decade. With huge increases in the share of welfare rolls made up of able-bodied employable applicants, the public seemed to decide that Canadian welfare recipients had overnight become wasteful, lazy, and deceitful.

One *Ottawa Citizen* columnist characterized a non-deserving welfare recipient, of which he claimed there were many, as a "ne'er-do-well spendthrift who wasted the last year drinking and gambling away a fortune in Las Vegas." A *Toronto Star* writer asked his readers why he should sympathize with people on welfare who, unable to manage their allowances, were then forced to go to food banks. Their financial management, he claimed, was inept. It didn't help that a professional welfare worker complained to the media that mothers on welfare sometimes wasted their allowances on extravagances like Pampers, inserts for baby bottles, and brand name baby food. These were popular sentiments. A Decima research poll in 1993 found Canadians in a sour mood about welfare, including strong feelings that recipients wasted their allowances.

Faced with a suspicious public, provincial and municipal welfare officials became as preoccupied with fraud in the 1990s as federal UI officials had been for over 15 years. The seed was sown when Metro Toronto's social services department established a telephone hotline (soon called the "snitch line") to allow Toronto residents to report those suspected of cheating the welfare system. While over 250 calls were taken on the first day of operation and an unknown number each day over the next weeks, the department finally had to admit that most allegations were unfounded. The situation had been "blown right out of proportion," according to the department head. Out of 780 calls received, investigators found evidence of fraud in three cases which cost taxpayers an estimated $9,334. An investigation responding to similar public pressure was conducted in Ottawa with the same results. The extent of fraud uncovered there represented only one percent of the welfare budget.

Despite these findings at the municipal level the Ontario social services minister announced a month later the government's intention of cracking down on fraud in the provincial caseload, generally made up of single mothers and people with disabilities. Other provinces followed suit. In BC the provincial government began working with the RCMP to track down fraud. Over 200 additional staff were hired; consideration was also being given to new requirements for welfare applicants including fingerprinting and photo ID. In Quebec the income security minister upgraded a number of welfare inspectors in response to public pressure about fraudulent use of the welfare system. Their new status gave them authority to ask neighbours, landlords, or employees at the corner store about the activities of welfare recipients under suspicion.

At the federal level an entire ethnic group was put under suspicion. Somali refugees, according to a leaked report, were ripping off Canada's welfare system and sending money back home to warlords. The report claimed an estimated 91 percent of Somalis were on welfare. They were part of an organized plan by Somali clan leaders who had arranged the mass export of refugees to Canada for the sole purpose of sending welfare cheques back home, or so the story went. When the public too readily accepted the report's authenticity Immigration Minister Sergio Marchi commented, more with resignation than surprise: "Unfortunately the public has come to believe that a large percentage of refugee claimants are engaged in some type of fraudulent activity. This is simply not the case."

There was no indication, however, that public attitudes were mellowing. In the spring of 1993 Alberta welfare employables were put to work maintaining parks or cleaning up rivers and highways. There was considerable support from the public. An *Edmonton Journal* editorial writer commented: "The citizens of this province hate poor people... They can't think of a punishment too severe, a humiliation too deep, for people on welfare." In the summer 700 Quebec mayors agreed that over 800,000 people who received unemployment insurance or welfare would soon be forced to do unpaid community work. These were firsts for Canada where "workfare" had previously been prohibited under the Canada Assistance Plan. In light of hardening public opinion, it appeared workfare would now be allowed. The federal government, working with focus groups in order to sense public opinion, had found that not only were group participants generally supportive of making people work for their welfare benefits, but the appeal for the idea seemed to stem from a feeling that it was a punitive measure and that punishment was in order.

Harsh attitudes translated into tougher welfare regulations in most provinces. BC "reformed" its welfare program, relying heavily on public opinion polls to ensure the new reforms would be palatable. Among other findings, polls showed that over 81 percent believed the BC government was not doing enough to stop welfare fraud.

Alberta and Ontario cut allowances drastically; Ontario also introduced its own workfare program and mandatory use of fingerprinting. (Over 60 percent of Canadians polled in 1996 favoured fingerprinting for welfare applicants.) New regulations in Quebec came down hard on single applicants. Across the country there was little support for people on welfare. An Environics poll asked Canadians which social program they would choose to cut if Canada reached a point where it could not afford the whole range. The welfare program was chosen more often than any other.

While welfare and UI recipients were increasingly unpopular, other poor Canadians also found themselves living in a society that was turning its back on sharing and compassion. A feature story in the *Globe and Mail* in 1997 highlighted the almost complete lack of concern about Native affairs on the part of Canadians. A year after the Oka crisis in the early 1990s only six percent of Canadians (surveyed in an Angus Reid poll) regarded Native affairs as a matter of significant interest. A year later the proportion was only four percent. By early 1997, just three months after the Royal Commission on Aboriginal Peoples had completed its extensive study and published its report, Native affairs were a matter of concern to only one percent of the population. Despite damaging descriptions of Aboriginal housing given in the royal commission report, for example, a 1997 Ekos poll found that respondents across the country gave the lowest priority to Aboriginal housing among all choices for increased federal spending. A federal member of Parliament from Saskatchewan, interviewed for the *Globe* article, revealed that it was not only lack of public concern for Aboriginal people, but a certain amount of hostility as well. His constituents, he said, had nothing to do with the injustices of the distant past reported in the pages of the royal commission report. And besides, he added, there is an abiding resentment toward Native people because "they can get by by doing sweet tweet."

There was also a growing sense in the 1990s that the poor could no longer continue to receive the same level of health care as all other Canadians. The issue of user fees had been theoretically laid to rest with the passage of the Canada Health Act in 1983. The terms of federal-provincial cost-sharing had required the provinces to operate *universal* medicare programs, that is, their programs were required to cover all residents, rich and poor, on uniform terms and conditions. User fees and extra billing were, therefore, in contravention of the legislation. The Act had been drafted in direct response to the 1980 recommendations of a review commission headed by former Supreme Court Justice Emmett Hall. The commission had warned:

> If extra-billing is permitted as a right and practised by physicians in their sole discretion, it will, over the years, destroy the program, creating in that downward path a two-tier system incompatible with the societal level which Canadians have attained.

Throughout the 1980s there was general compliance with the requirement of universality. Roughly 80 percent of Canadians polled the year the Canada Health Act took effect were against extra-billing and user fees.

Rising demands on the health care system, however, changed public attitudes. A concern that surfaced as costs rose was the alleged misuse of the system by Canadians who did not really need services. In Quebec, Senator Claude Castonguay, often called the father of Quebec medicare, recommended that the federal government relax the requirement of the Canada Health Act and allow some types of user fees. User fees, he claimed, "would make consumers think twice about whether they need certain services." In Alberta, the government announced it would press the federal health minister for Canada Health Act changes to allow doctors to charge a fee to patients for every office visit. In other words, according to user fee supporters, there seemed to be a considerable amount of minor hypochondria among Canadians, and user fees across the board would reduce it. Low-income Canadians who could not afford user fees would presumably be cured of their hypochondria in a hurry, while those who could afford the fees might still be able to waste the doctor's time if that was the way they wanted to spend an afternoon.

The real reason behind the pressure for user fees was that governments of the 1990s at both the federal and provincial levels were trying to balance budgets. Whether hypochondria was truly an epidemic or not, health care spending had to be controlled as did other government spending. As funding failed to keep pace with rising health care costs in most provinces, the level of care suffered and people were waiting longer and longer periods for medical and hospital service. User fees would inject new funds and restore the level of service. Since they were not permissible under the Canada Health Act, however, Canadians who wanted a higher quality and more responsive service had to look to other solutions.

The solution of private health care for middle- and upper-income Canadians became increasingly popular, first among professionals in the health field and, soon after, among the general public. The Canadian Medical Association passed a resolution at its 1992 annual meeting to ask for a change in the Canada Health Act so that high-income earners could pay part of their health care. The following year a study conducted by the Fraser Institute in BC recommended that wealthy Canadians should be allowed to go to the head of queues for medical treatment if they paid the full cost. By the mid-1990s the medicare system was so strained that eight out of ten Canadians polled by *Maclean's* magazine said they expected a two-tier health system in Canada within ten years with private care for those who can afford it and medicare for those who cannot. Roughly 47 percent found this solution acceptable. A similar finding came out of an Angus Reid poll in BC earlier in the year; half the population of that province was of the opinion that some form of private involvement in health care was required.

By 1999 there was even stronger support for private health care. A Pollara survey found that access to medicare was considered a serious problem. More and more Canadians were reaching the conclusion that patients were not getting treated quickly enough in the public system. A substantial majority (83 percent) of Canadians believed medicare was losing ground or simply standing still in solving the problem of access. Over 73 percent believed that if timely access to health services was not available Canadians should have the option of using private facilities.

Less assistance to the unemployed and user fees for the sick are only two examples of the harsher attitudes of Canadians as the 20th century came to a close. A new atmosphere pervaded public discourse. Major newspapers began to satisfy the appetites of tough-minded readers with special poor-bashing columnists. Lead editorials followed up with more sane and mature comment for those who were more educated but just as anxious to get tough with down-and-out Canadians. Letter writers railed at their fellow citizens who weren't carrying their weight.

What had happened over 20 years was the emergence of self-reliance as one of the dominant values of Canadians. It was, to be more accurate, a rediscovery of a strongly held Canadian belief dating back to the late 19th and early 20th centuries While it might be difficult to find similarities between the scattered and sparse Canadian population of five million in 1900 and the highly urban population of almost 30 million in 2000, both had poor in their midst and considered their demands a potential drain on limited resources and a barrier to economic progress. In 1900, while it was characteristic of struggling farmers to help each other at every stage of the agricultural cycle, they were less interested in helping the poor in the industrial sector. They understood unexpected years of crop failure better than they understood unexpected years of recession that were typical of industrialization. Though they lobbied for and were given government farm subsidies to help them through the lean years, of which there were many, they considered themselves self-sufficient and expected everyone else to be the same. Industrialists, on the other hand, had other reasons to hold self-reliance in high regard. It was necessary to have a certain amount of stigma attached to being dependent in order to maintain a willing workforce for the needs of industry which was still in its infancy. Self-reliance rather than dependence was already highly valued in predominantly agricultural Canada—it was made to order for the growing industrial sector.

In the last two decades of the 20th century Canadians again saw the dependence of the poor as a potential threat to the economic strength of the country. There had been considerable growth in the Canadian social conscience in the intervening years—a concern for the poor and a willingness to share the national product. But public attitudes changed. Today we tolerate few special circumstances that would warrant our help. If we work, we want our neighbours to work regardless of their individual circumstances. If we have managed to be self-reliant, we want our neighbours to manage, regardless of their capacity for self-reliance. If *we* can make it—and make it on our own—why can't everyone? Unfortunately the self-made man (or woman) is a piece of North American fiction. The true story is far less heroic. We make it with the help of parents during our dependent childhood years, with the help of teachers lifting us out of illiteracy and ignorance, with the help of the first employer who hired us when we had no work experience, and with some small assistance from the hand of fate.

The truth is human society is built on life cycles of relative dependence and independence, from childhood years though working years to old age. Periods of health and sickness, good fortune and bad fortune, are also thrown in. Without dependence the role of helping disappears from social life and we are all, especially the helpers, a little the worse for it. Today helping is on its way out. Dependence has no place in the new competitive international economy. To make things work, we must all act in our own selfish interests, pull our own weight, give a good sound kick to those who won't do the same. The poor, among them the homeless, will have to look after themselves whether that is a realistic expectation or not. There is little in the way of goodwill in the hearts of Canadians.

CHAPTER 10

Natural Selection at Work

The history of the world, back to its earliest beginnings, is filled with rather remarkable examples of human adaptation to a sometimes unfriendly natural environment, not the least of which was the capacity to solve the basic survival need for shelter. From the tropical zone of Africa, where the earliest traces of primitive man were discovered, to the temperate zones stretching across Europe, Asia, Australia, and North America, the challenges of rain and cold were overcome by a human species intent on surviving.

Even early hunting and gathering societies, though nomadic, managed to create temporary shelters. At each temporary "home base" or campsite, according to anthropologists, lean-tos or dome-shaped huts were built beside each outdoor family hearth. Later, probably about 20,000 to 15,000 years ago, agricultural societies put up more permanent houses as settlement in villages became a way of life in old areas of the world. Houses in these permanent settlements have been described by archaeologists as "careful, substantial architecture," meant to last. Some were more permanent versions of the round dwellings of the nomads; later village houses were rectangular, enclosing the hearth and separate areas for living and for food storage.

Faced with colder climates, the early inhabitants of northern Europe and Asia had additional challenges. Winter settlement sites were characterized by solidly built houses with two or three fireplaces and heavy turf roofs; houses at summer settlement sites were light structures of birchbark, usually without interior fireplaces.

Besides these semi-nomadic societies whose lives alternated

between two or three almost-permanent seasonal sites, more classic hunting and gathering societies also inhabited northern Europe and Asia as far east as Siberia. These nomads acclimatized to the cold climate without benefit of solid permanent shelter. Clothed in animal skins or furs, they had to be, or soon became, robust and resourceful people. It is generally believed that one or two, or perhaps several, of these nomadic societies crossed the Bering land bridge between Asia and Alaska (just at the edge of the Arctic Circle) about 25,000 years ago and became the earliest North American inhabitants, ancestors of today's aboriginal peoples.

If they had hoped for a more hospitable climate in the new land they were disappointed. Many migrated south along the Pacific coast. Those who remained north of the 49th parallel of latitude became the first Canadians. They kept warm during Canada's frigid winters in wigwams and tepees. Some nomadic societies later settled in agricultural villages where they kept warm in longhouses that sheltered several family units with individual hearths.

European settlers who arrived thousands of years later could not match their stamina. Indeed many perished in the cold. But over the next 400 years settlers from Europe and eventually from other continents also became acclimatized. With technological advances, they built and heated substantial houses that allowed them to survive the brutal Canadian winters.

From the beginning of human migration into northern climates of the world, one cannot find any society that allowed even a small portion of its people to live without shelter in the winter. It has been left to late 20th-century and early 21st-century societies to claim this dubious achievement. Whether such indifference has been the product of a sophistication lacking in earlier cultures is open to debate. It is true the advances of modern society are unparalleled in the roughly 75,000 years of the existence of modern man. It is also possible "survival" issues are now too basic for the public agenda. Possibly, too, there is still some doubt that people can die in Canada if they have to live without shelter during the winter. Yet there is considerable evidence that Canadians without shelter can and do die in average January temperatures of minus 21 degrees Celsius in prairie cities and minus 15 in cities of Quebec and Ontario.

In early February 2000—at about four in the morning when

the mercury is at its lowest—the body of a 55-year-old homeless man was found lying under a bench near the lower locks of the Rideau Canal in Ottawa. It was not at an isolated stretch of the canal, but in the heart of the city behind the Château Laurier Hotel, one of Ottawa's pride and joy landmarks. So indeed is the Rideau Canal itself, a tourist attraction that tries to be a friendly "people" place to all who use its recreational paths, but it was not so friendly that night. Dressed in heavy winter clothing, homeless Robert Coté still could not make it through the night. He froze to death. A year earlier Lynn Maureen Bluecloud died on the other side of the canal, her frozen body found in the bush on a cold morning in late February. A Native woman, she was five months pregnant.

Even as they looked for the family of Robert Coté, Ottawa police were still trying to unravel the death of a man in his thirties whose frozen body was found two days earlier in a suburban industrial park. In a bizarre twist, a police dog on a training exercise led his handler to the unidentified man's body which had apparently lain in an abandoned, unheated shed for several days. The temperature in Ottawa in the week prior to the discovery averaged minus 18 degrees Celsius.

The same bitter cold snap took the life of a homeless man a few days earlier in Montreal where overnight temperatures were officially recorded as minus 51 degrees Celsius with windchill. In the early morning an office worker, hurrying to get out of the cold herself, initially ignored Gino Laplante's calls for help as he lay wrapped in a sleeping bag outside the Place d'Armes metro station. When the worker returned with emergency help minutes later it was too late and there was little doubt it had been too late when she first saw him. Before his death the 38-year-old man suffered from mental illness. He was being helped to live outside the mental hospital through a community treatment program. It was clear, however, he was not ready to be on his own, despite many personal contacts with program staff.

Residents of Toronto were shocked in the winter of 1999 when the frozen body of an unidentified homeless man was found curled up on top of a heat vent on a downtown street. Perhaps mistakenly he believed the warmth of the heat vent would protect him against the minus 8 degrees Celsius temperature in Toronto that night, a temperature that would have been the envy of other cities in Canada. In the morning a hydro worker found his body buried under old blankets, sleeping bags, and pieces of cardboard. An unopened can of corn was among his meager possessions.

The irony of the tragedy occurring just a few floors below the posh offices of Ontario Premier Mike Harris was not lost on the media. In light of the publicity, provincial MPs joined others at the heat vent a few days later to mourn the passing of the 52-year-old homeless man. Within a year, however, the same MPs passed legislation intended to make Ontario streets safer, not for the homeless who might freeze to death, but for more fortunate residents of Ontario who were becoming increasingly irritated with these visible reminders of poverty in their midst.

Just two weeks before the Toronto air-vent tragedy, the frozen body of a homeless man was found in Calgary in a park near the Calgary Zoo. Jens Drape was 37 years old. Friends who traced him to the park when he failed to show up at an emergency shelter during the night reported that he had been close to securing an apartment a few weeks earlier. With the help of the Calgary Homeless Foundation he had even obtained the necessary security deposit, but at the last minute the landlord had changed his mind. Drinking in the park at minus 16 degrees Celsius, he apparently drifted off to sleep. "He didn't move," said one of the friends who found his body, "he was frozen solid."

The early winter months of 1997-98 were fatal for two homeless men in greater Toronto. In November Michael Faithorne, 41, froze to death in the stairwell of a parking garage near Queen Street West and Jameson. His body was found wrapped in a sleeping bag. The temperature had not even dropped below minus 15 degrees Celsius, the point at which Metro Toronto implemented its "extreme cold alert" program.

At the other end of the city an unidentified middle-aged homeless man froze to death in a Scarborough ravine. A man walking his dog found the body on the east shore of a creek where it lay huddled under a blue tarp that had failed to keep him alive.

In the same month the frozen body of an unidentified homeless man was found by a Christmas shopper in a parking lot in downtown Montreal. Wrapped in a sleeping bag, the man was believed to be

71 years of age. The parking lot behind the Cinéma Parisien on Ste-Catherine Street was just a few feet away from some of the city's finest stores where thousands of Montrealers were doing their last-minute shopping three days before Christmas. The overnight temperature had been minus 16 degrees Celsius.

These three were not the only homeless Canadians who froze to death in 1997. In February William Hunta, 74, died near the Don Valley Parkway in Toronto, his body discovered on the loading dock of an abandoned and unheated industrial building. Police believed he may have been living for some time under the nearby Richmond Street bridge.

In January a much younger man, Garland Sheppard, 34, also froze to death. It is perhaps revealing that police initially described him as middle-aged. His body was found on the third floor of an open-air parking garage in downtown Toronto where he had spent the night at minus 17 degrees Celsius. Empty liquor bottles, sleeping bags, and blankets were found nearby, none of which had been enough to get Sheppard through the night.

In the winter of 1996 three homeless men died in Toronto in a four-week period. Eugene Upper, 56 years old, was found dead in a Spadina Avenue bus shelter in the early hours of a cold January day. He had been drinking heavily, refused to be helped to a shelter during the night by a street worker, and froze to death by morning. One of his drinking friends reported that Upper wanted two things badly in the last months of his life—to find housing and to quit drinking. Both goals, however, had escaped him.

Three weeks later the frozen body of a 41-year-old homeless man, Mirsalah-Aldin Kompani, was found underneath the eastbound ramp to the Gardiner Expressway at Bay Street. His hands were frozen to his face and his shoes were tucked under his arm as if he feared, according to a *Toronto Star* reporter, they might be stolen while he slept.

No one could say how long he had lived under the bridge in a small lean-to made from a car hood and scraps of lumber. Kompani, a refugee, had been treated for mental illness in the past, but had been refused admission by two different hospital psychiatrists in Toronto more than a year previously. At a later inquest both doctors admitted they believed Kompani's request for hospital admission was simply a request for shelter. It was clearly not the kind of basic need they had been trained to provide.

A third homeless man died the day after the discovery of Komani's body. Irwin Anderson, a Native man 63 years old, froze to death in the doorway of a college for cosmeticians in Toronto's east end. The temperature overnight, although forecast at minus 23 degrees Celsius, had only dropped to minus 16. Arriving to open the college, a woman found his body curled up in the stairwell to the door. According to staff at the Native centre (some distance away), Anderson had been evicted from his apartment the previous summer and had been living on the streets ever since.

A lengthy inquest into the deaths of Anderson, Upper, and Kompani raised the awareness of Torontonians about risks of freezing among the homeless. The coroner, however, was not prepared to blame the fate of the three men on lack of shelter; instead he blamed a "compromised mental state" and charged the jury to arrive at that finding. In a remarkable demonstration of independence the five-member jury rejected his advice and identified homelessness as a major contributing circumstance to the three deaths. Jury members issued 47 recommendations for public action to ensure access to housing for the homeless.

Homeless people can also die of the cold in British Columbia. Following a cold weekend in December of 1994 early-morning commuters to Vancouver heard on their car radios that the body of a 45-year-old homeless woman had been found behind a Langley hotel. Two teenagers discovered the body frozen beneath a sheet of ice in the flooded gravel parking lot. Police were forced to use axes to chip the unidentified woman's body out of the frozen water. Normal Vancouver temperatures of near zero Celsius had dipped to minus 8 degrees during the night. It was believed the woman died about 2 a.m.

In Prince Rupert during the same cold snap a 58-year-old man froze to death near the waterfront. He had been drinking, finally falling asleep in the minus 10 degrees temperature.

Less than a month later, following a record-breaking cold spell in Toronto, the frozen body of a homeless man was found sprawled in the snow in the rear parking lot of an Etobicoke hotel. Dale Phillips was 55 years old. Perhaps more fortunate, though one could argue otherwise, a homeless man in Thunder Bay lost both his legs to frostbite a month earlier. The unidentified man had been sleeping in an unheated shack.

The good cheer of the Christmas season does not always spread to the homeless. On Boxing Day in 1992 Alister Letendre's frozen body was discovered in an alley behind a 4th Avenue store in Calgary. Letendre, 45 and homeless, had fallen asleep outdoors in a temperature of minus 28 degrees Celsius.

A year earlier the Christmas period was also a tragic time for a Toronto homeless woman who was found frozen and unconscious by security guards in a downtown parking garage. Jennie Balcombe, who was 66 years old and mentally ill, was known to churches and shelters in the area where she often found sanctuary from the cold. That night, however, when the overnight low reached minus 15 degrees Celsius, she froze to death without shelter, her possessions in a shopping cart that was always with her.

We would be overwhelmed and immobilized if we made ourselves responsible for the death, or even the tragic life, of every homeless stranger in the world. Perhaps we could start with just those in Canada who are arguably more within reach. We could start by recognizing that the homeless are the most destitute of our poor. We could move, as a next step, to acknowledging their right to use public places to remind us of their poverty. To turn this around, in fact, we could ask what rule of modern society has stipulated that the non-poor have exclusive right to public places or indeed the right to decide who can be visible and who cannot and who can speak and who cannot in places meant for everyone.

There are good reasons for minimizing disorderliness (or so-called "street disorder") in our urban centres, but we have to question any premise that turns street begging into disorderly behaviour. Instead, as one specialist in the field of ethics points out, "by addressing other members of society with a plea for help, the beggar is challenging society for recognition and is, in the process, challenging the stigma which attaches to poverty and exclusion."[1] Annoying though that challenge may be as we walk along downtown streets looking for places to spend our money, surely we can give those who are asking for help the right to ask.

There are other policies we have put in place that also need to be undone. We need to challenge city planning policies in our major metropolitan areas that allow the revitalization of inner cities at the expense of affordable housing for the poor. This is not an easy task, given the sanctity of property values and the powerful voice of the middle class in determining civic policies.

If the voices of the poor have not been heard in the steady disappearance of low-rent housing units, it is because we have drowned them out. Our demands for urban core areas that reduce the mix of income groups have put our major cities at risk of losing their sense of community, their character, and even their authenticity as living places that reflect the whole of society. If we don't want the poor on our public downtown streets, surely we can provide rooms and apartments for them to rent in our inner cities.

It means putting a stop to demolitions and instead making use of existing housing stock as it becomes available for low-income units. But primarily it means confronting the fears of property owners and educating them about the negligible effect of income mixing on property values. It has already been demonstrated in some communities.

As we head into the 21st century Canadian society still has a long way to go in treating its mentally ill with respect and compassion. We are no further ahead than we were in the 19th century when cost-effectiveness dictated the development of larger and larger institutions with smaller and smaller staffs. In the end, both efficiencies contributed to almost criminal neglect. Today we turn the mentally ill onto the streets in the name of rehabilitation, but we have still managed to let cost-effectiveness translate into neglect. We have failed to make non-institutional rehabilitation work because savings from closing institutions were not redirected at services for those closed out.

The problem of treatment for the mentally ill is not insoluble. We have to start by saying to ourselves every day, three times a day, *many cannot make it on their own in the community.* When we are finally convinced of that reality we can feel more comfortable about small institutions, hopefully part of local general hospitals, where the chronic mentally ill can be provided with the special care they need. We need to be constantly vigilant that cost-effectiveness is not allowed to enlarge these small settings or provide an excuse for understaffing. The non-chronic mentally ill can, of course, be helped in the community and, in fact, the community is probably the best place for them. But once again they cannot be helped without adequate numbers of outreach staff or adequate community support services (such as help with housing).

The treatment of both chronic and non-chronic mentally ill patients requires public spending. We have been unwilling to make these expenditures in the past. Did we fail to identify with this group because they were outside our personal experience? Certainly many families kept them hidden, and institutions kept them behind walls. But all that has changed; we see mentally ill Canadians every day on our city sidewalks. It would be a fortunate circumstance for them, and clearly a step forward in our own development, if we could now identify more closely with their plight. In the final analysis, they are ill. At least we have come that far in our thinking. It is time to give them the treatment we normally provide for the ill.

There are other actions that need undoing. We can wring our hands in despair about the abandonment of the rental housing market by private-sector builders, but the truth is overregulation of the home building industry has had our blessing.

Many studies have shown that middle-income renters benefit most from rent control so perhaps it is time for us to examine the consequences for low-income renters, the most damaging of which has been that private builders have pulled out of an unattractive market. Low-income renters are the ones paying the price as affordable housing disappears. Landlord-and-tenant legislation also needs to be re-examined to determine whether the balance between the rights of the landlord and the rights of the tenant has been tipped so much in favour of the tenant that landlords are deciding they can find less stressful ways to make a living.

At best, and even with reforms to building codes, the private sector has difficulty creating rental housing at costs that can be covered by the low rents the poor can afford. Even if some investors could be lured back into the market by reducing overregulation and tax disincentives, the supply of low-rent units would not grow immediately. The private building industry, characterized by lags between investment and final product, is notoriously slow-moving. The reduction in regulation, however, needs to go ahead. If the private rental supply begins to increase as a result, low-income renters can compete with others in the private housing market. They will need financial help to compete.

Current shelter allowances for social assistance recipients are too low now and would be even more out of line by the time supply increases. Moreover, the shelter allowance programs available in a few provinces for the working poor (as compared with social assistance recipients) are not reaching many who need them. The whole shelter allowance system needs expansion and enrichment. It would require considerable public expenditure but, of all housing solutions, it is probably the least expensive.

The private sector cannot begin to provide all low-income housing needs. Our responsibility to the homeless involves renewed funding of social housing. Once again existing housing stock can be put to better use in re-introducing public investment in low-income housing, but what is needed even more is the willingness of taxpayers to move it to the top of the list of public priorities. It has not been the case in the 1980s and 1990s, and this public unwillingness has contributed directly to the rapidly increasing number of homeless.

Growing poverty and growing public indifference have gone hand in hand during this period. It is an unhappy, even tragic, combination. And the impetus for action is still missing. When we are criticized by a United Nations committee for the neglect of our Aboriginal people, our lone-parent families, and our other poor, we huff and puff and declare their statistics outdated. Perhaps some of the members of the UN committee walked along Elgin Street in Ottawa or Bloor Street in Toronto or Hastings Street in Vancouver in addition to looking at statistics.

What may be worse than indifference is an increasingly harsh public attitude toward the poor that prompts us to cut back on income programs, like employment insurance and welfare, that may actually help them. To point out that this is counter-productive in light of increasing poverty in Canada seems obvious. It is not only counter-productive; it has made a major contribution to the growing number of poor and homeless. Nonetheless it warrants repeating that less income assistance puts people on the street.

Solutions for homelessness are not out of reach. What may be out of reach, however, is public willingness to act when many of the solutions involve looking out for the needs of the homeless alongside our own. If we could see ourselves in something of a public guardian role, it could work. Canadians have been known to rise to such occasions in the past. If that role is beyond us today, the homeless will stay in that separate world of theirs, and we will stay in ours.

Appendix

SOCIO-ECONOMIC CHANGES, INNER CITIES, 1971-1996
Percentages

	1971		1996	
	INNER CITY	WHOLE CITY	INNER CITY	WHOLE CITY
Ottawa				
University completion*	10	10	39	29
Holding white-collar jobs**	42	47	91	87
Halifax				
University completion	9	7	41	26
Holding white-collar jobs	52	52	92	84
Toronto				
University completion	8	7	32	24
Holding white-collar jobs	38	39	84	79
Montreal				
University completion	5	6	32	23
Holding white-collar jobs	37	40	86	79
Vancouver				
University completion	7	6	31	24
Holding white-collar jobs	42	42	85	80

* Percent of university completion among adult population

** Percent of managerial, professional, and white-collar jobs held of all jobs held

Statistics Canada, *Census of Canada, Population and Housing Characteristics by Census Tracts*, 1971 and 1996.

Endnotes

Chapter 1
1. The homeless have been found in bus and railroad stations, on steam grates, in doorways and vestibules, in cardboard boxes, and in abandoned cars.
2. For example, Census of Canada, P. Filion and T. Bunting, *Affordability of Housing in Canada*, 1990, and Canada Mortgage and Housing, *CORE: Housing Need in Canada*, 1991.
3. *Vancouver Sun*, "New Westminster Targets Nuisance," May 7, 1998, p. B3.
4. *Time*, "Buddy, Can You Spare a Dime?" February 12, 1990, p. 51.
5. Henry Miller, *On the Fringe, The Dispossessed in America*, 1991.

Chapter 2
1. Statistics Canada, *Historical Statistics of Canada*, 1983.
2. *Westboro, Ottawa's Westmount, an illustrative number devoted to its past, present and future growth*, 1913.
3. R. Harris and G.J. Pratt, "The Meaning of Home, Home Ownership, and Public Policy," in *The Changing Social Geography of Canadian Cities*, eds. L.S. Bourne and D.F. Ley, 1993.

Chapter 3
1. Information on urban renewal projects is taken from CMHC Annual Reports, 1949 to 1975.
2. Canada, *Report of the Task Force on Housing and Urban Development*, 1969.
3. *Intruders* (Toronto: McGraw-Hill, 1976.)
4. Detailed figures are given in the Appendix. Comparative data, 1971 and 1996, are taken from Statistics Canada, Census of Canada, *Population and Housing Characteristics by Census Tracts*.

Chapter 4
1. Presidential address of T.J.W. Burgess to the Royal Society of Canada given on May 25, 1898, and entitled "A Historical Sketch of our Canadian Institutions for the Insane."
2. Reported in Daniel Brock, *History of the County of Middlesex, Canada*, 1972, and Glenn J. Lockwood, *Beckwith, Irish and Scottish Identities in a Canadian Community*, 1991.

3. Upper Canada Sundries, February 16, 1839, quoted in Richard Splane, *Social Welfare in Ontario 1791-1893*, 1965.
4. H.M. Hurd, *The Institutional Care of the Insane in the United States and Canada*, 1973, p. 204.
5. Hurd, p. 253.
6. Hurd, p. 79.
7. Burgess, "A Historical Sketch of our Canadian Institutions for the Insane," p. 53.

Chapter 5
1. According to the Clarke Institute of Psychiatry, the main diagnostic groupings of the chronic population in mental hospitals in the 1970s, excluding mental retardation and epilepsy, were schizophrenia, chronic affective disorder, chronic brain syndrome, and severe neurotic and personality disorders, schizophrenia being the predominant disorder.
2. A.B. Johnson, *Out of Bedlam, The Truth About Deinstitutionalization*, 1990, pp. 79-80.

Chapter 6
1. Christopher Hauch, *Coping Strategies and Street Life: The Ethnography of Winnipeg's Skid Row Region*, 1985.
2. Most of these facts are from the National Council on Welfare's *Poverty Profile 1997*. Statistics Canada's *Lone Parent Families in Canada*, 1992, also provided information.
3. The CMHC study, *No Room of Her Own: A Literature Review on Women and Homelessness*, was conducted by Sylvia Novac, Joyce Brown, and Carmen Bourbonnais.
4. Patrick Falconer, author of the article "The Overlooked of the Neglected: Native Single Mothers in Major Cities of the Prairies," also warns that the unemployment and hardship of Native single parents in the cities may affect the probability of their children completing high school. Given the predominance of lone-parent families among Native urban families, this could have a long-term effect on the future of the whole urban Native community.

Chapter 7
1. This restriction referred to non-profit non-cooperative housing rather than cooperative housing. Most non-profit non-cooperative housing was provided by municipal governments with federal assistance under global agreements with the provinces. Federal arrangements with cooperative housing corporations, on the other hand, were unilateral and their mixed-income projects continued to be funded for another six years.

Chapter 8
1. Housing statistics in this chapter are taken from Canada Mortgage and Housing statistical and market survey reports.
2. In the 2000 federal budget the GST rebate was finally extended to purchasers of rental property.

3. Housing starts, in general, were down over the same period in Canada and BC (22 percent and 35 percent respectively), but the drop in rental housing starts was significantly greater.

4. Roger Greenberg, "The Key to New Housing: Government Must Lower Barriers to Private-sector Investment," *Ottawa Citizen*, September 6, 1995.

5. Harry M. Kitchen, *Property Taxation in Canada*, 1992.

6. Donald H.L. Lamont, *Residential Tenancies*, 1993, p. 5.

7. Steve Pomeroy, *Residualization of Rental Tenure: Attitudes of Private Landlords Toward Housing Low-income Households*, 1998.

Chapter 9
1. Evidence of changing public attitudes described in this chapter can be found in more detail in Barbara Murphy, *The Ugly Canadian: The Rise and Fall of a Caring Society*, 1999.

Chapter 10
1. Arthur Schafer, *Down and Out in Winnipeg and Toronto: The Ethics of Legislating Against Panhandling*, 1998.

Selected Bibliography

Books and Journals

Allderidge, Patricia, "Hospitals, Madhouses, and Asylums," *British Journal of Psychiatry*, vol. 134, 1979.

Allodi, F.A. and H.B. Kedward, "The Vanishing Chronic," *Canadian Journal of Public Health*, vol. 64, 1973.

Allodi, F.A. and H.B. Kedward, "Evolution of the Mental Hospital in Canada," *Canadian Journal of Public Health*, vol. 68, 1977.

Archer, John, "A History of Housing Standards," *Habitat*, vol. 24, 1981.

Artibise, Alan F.J., *Winnipeg: A Social History of Urban Growth, 1874-1914* (Montreal: McGill-Queen's University Press, 1975).

Bacher, John A., *Keeping to the Marketplace, The Evolution of Canadian Housing Policy* (Montreal: McGill-Queen's University Press, 1993).

Bairstow, Dale, *Reaching Out for Help: Manitoba's Homeless in 1987,* prepared for the Manitoba Ministry of Housing (Winnipeg, 1987).

Bean, Philip and Patricia Mounser, *Discharged from Mental Hospitals* (London: Macmillan, 1993).

Beavis, Mary Ann et al., *Literature Review: Aboriginal Peoples and Homelessness,* Canada Mortgage and Housing (Ottawa, 1997).

Begin, Patricia, *Homelessness in Canada,* Library of Parliament, Research Division (Ottawa, 1996).

Blakely, Phyllis, *Glimpses of Halifax* (Belleville: Mika Publishing, 1973).

Bourne, Larry and David F. Ley, eds., *The Changing Social Geography of Canadian Cities* (Montreal: McGill-Queen's University Press, 1993).

Brock, Daniel, *History of the County of Middlesex, Canada* (Belleville: Mika Publishing, 1972).

Bunting, Trudi and P. Filion, eds., *The Changing Canadian Inner City* (Waterloo: University of Waterloo, 1988).

Burgess, T.J.W., "A Historical Sketch of our Canadian Institutions for the Insane," *Transactions of the Royal Society of Canada,* Section IV, 1898.

Canada, *House of Commons Debates,* June 23, 1975; February 2, 1977; November 9, 1978; June 1, 1989.

Canada, *Report of Federal Task Force on Housing and Urban Development* (Ottawa, 1969).

Canada, *Report of Royal Commission on Aboriginal Peoples* (Ottawa, 1996).

Canada, Dominion Bureau of Statistics, *Mental Institutions, 1946-1958,* cat. 83-204.

Canada Mortgage and Housing, *CORE: Housing Need in Canada* (Ottawa, 1991).

Canada, Statistics Canada, *Historical Statistics of Canada,* 1983.

Canada, Statistics Canada, *Lone Parent Families in Canada,* cat. 89-522E, 1992.

Canada, Statistics Canada, Census of Canada, *Population and Housing Characteristics by Census Tracts,* 1971 and 1996.

Canada Year Book, 11-202, Motor Vehicles Registered in Canada (Ottawa, 1948).

Canadian Council on Social Development, *A Review of Canadian Social Housing Policy* (Ottawa, 1977).

Canadian Home Builders' Association, *Developing a Strategy for Housing Assistance in Canada* (Ottawa, 1999).

Canadian Home Builders' Association, *Pulse Survey* (Ottawa, Spring/summer, 1999).

Canadian Mental Health Association, *More for the Mind* (Ottawa: 1963).

Canu, Linda, *A Bold Step Forward, The History of the Fundy Mental Health Centre, Wolfville, N.S.* (Fundy Mental Health Foundation, 1986).

Census of Canada, P. Filion and T. Bunting, *Affordability of Housing in Canada,* 1990.

City of Calgary, *Count of Homeless Persons in Downtown Calgary,* 1998.

Clatworthy, Stewart, *Migration and Mobility of Canada's Aboriginal Population,* Canada Mortgage and Housing (Ottawa, 1996).

Dear, Michael and Jennifer Wolch, *Landscapes of Despair, From Deinstitutionalization to Homelessness* (Cambridge: Polity Press, 1987).

Edmonton Task Force on Homelessness, *Homelessness in Edmonton, A Call to Action,* 1998.

Erickson, Paul A. *Halifax's North End* (Huntsport: Lancelot Press, 1986).

Evenden, L.J. "Shaping the Vancouver Suburbs," in *Vancouver: Western Metropolis,* eds. L. J. Evenden, Western Geographical Series, vol. 16 (Victoria: University of Victoria, 1978).

Fakhruddin, A.K.M. et al., "A Five-Year Outcome of Discharged Chronic Psychiatric Patients," *Canadian Psychiatric Association Journal,* vol. 17, 1972.

Falconer, Patrick, "The Overlooked of the Neglected: Native Single Mothers in Major Cities in the Prairies," in *The Political Economy of Manitoba,* eds. J. Silver, J. Hull (Regina: Canadian Plains Research Center, 1990).

Fallis, George and Alex Murray, eds., *Housing the Homeless and Poor: New Partnerships Among the Private, Public and Third Sectors* (Toronto: University of Toronto Press, 1990).

Fallis, George and Lawrence Smith, "Tax Reform and Residential Real Estate," in Jack Mintz and John Whalley, eds., *The Economic Impacts of Tax Reform* (Toronto: Canadian Tax Foundation, 1989).

Fallis, George et al., *Home Remedies, Rethinking Canadian Housing Policy,* C.D. Howe Institute (Ottawa, 1995).

Foran, Max, "Land Development Patterns in Calgary 1845-1945," in A.F.J. Artibise and Gilbert A. Stelter, eds., *The Usable Urban Past: Planning and Politics in the Modern Canadian City* (Toronto, 1979).

Forward, Charles, "The Immortality of a Fashionable Residential District, The Uplands," in *Residential and Neighbourhood Studies in Victoria,* Charles Forward, ed., Western Geographical Series, vol. 5 (Victoria: University of Victoria, 1973).

Gerecke, Kent, ed., *The Canadian City* (Montreal: Black Rose Books, 1991).

Griffen, J.D. and C. Greenland, "Institutional Care of the Mentally Disordered in Canada—A 17th Century Record," *Canadian Journal of Psychiatry,* vol. 26, 1981.

Gubbay, A., *Montreal, the Mountain and the River* (Montreal: Trillium Books, 1981).

Gubbay, A., and S. Hooff, *Montreal's Little Mountain, A Portrait of Westmount* (Montreal: Ross Ellis, 1979).

Hanna, David B., "Creation of an Early Victorian Suburb in Montreal," in Gilbert A. Stelter, ed., *Cities and Urbanization* (Toronto: Copp Clark Pitman, 1990).

Hardwick, Walter G., *Vancouver* (Don Mills: Collier-Macmillan, 1974).

Hauch, Christopher, *Coping Strategies and Street Life: The Ethnography of Winnipeg's Skid Row Region,* University of Winnipeg Institute of Urban Studies (1985).

Herjanic M. et al., "The Chronic Patient in the Community, A Two-Year Follow-up of 338 Chronic Patients," *Canadian Psychiatric Association Journal*, vol. 13, 1968.

Heseltine, G.F., *Toward a Blueprint for Change: A Mental Health Policy Program Perspective* (Toronto: Ontario Ministry of Health, 1983).

Homelessness Action Task Force, *Taking Responsibility for Homelessness, An Action Plan for Toronto* (Toronto, 1999).

Hurd, H.M. *The Institutional Care of the Insane in the United States and Canada* (New York: Arno Press, 1973).

Isaac, Rael Jean and Virginia Armat, *Madness in the Streets: How Psychiatry and the Law Abandoned the Mentally Ill* (New York: Free Press, 1990).

Jackson, B.G., *Social Worlds in Transition, Neighbourhood Change in Grandview-Woodland, Vancouver*, unpublished Master's thesis, University of British Columbia, 1986.

Johnson, Ann B., *Out of Bedlam, The Truth About Deinstitutionalization* (New York: Basic Books, 1990).

Jones, A.E., *Beginnings of Canadian Government Housing Policy 1918-1924,* Centre for Social Welfare Studies, Carleton University (Ottawa, 1978).

Jones, Kathleen, *Mental Health and Social Policy 1845-1959* (London: Routledge and Kegan Paul, 1960).

Kedward, H.B. et al., "The Evaluation of Chronic Psychiatric Care," *Canadian Medical Association Journal,* vol. 110, 1974.

Kerr, D. et al., *Canada's Aboriginal Population 1981-1991*, Canada Mortgage and Housing (Ottawa, 1996).

Kitchen, Harry M., *Property Taxation in Canada,* Canadian Tax Foundation, Canadian Tax Paper No. 92 (Ottawa, 1992).

Lamont, Donald H.L. *Residential Tenancies* (Toronto: Carswell, 1993).

Lampert, Greg, *Review of Recent Reports on the Rental Market in Canada*, prepared for Canadian Home Builders' Association (Ottawa, 1999).

Ley, David, *Gentrification in Canadian Inner Cities: Patterns, Analysis, Impacts and Policy*, Canada Mortgage and Housing (October, 1985).

Lockwood, Glenn J., *Beckwith, Irish and Scottish Identities in a Canadian Community* (Carleton Place, ON: Township of Beckwith, 1991).

Lum, Sophia, *Residential Redevelopment in the Inner City of Vancouver, A Case Study of Fairview Slopes,* unpublished Master's thesis, Queen's University, 1984.

McLaughlin, MaryAnn, *Homelessness in Canada, The Report of the National Inquiry,* Canadian Council on Social Development (Ottawa, 1987).

Miller, Henry, *On the Fringe, The Dispossessed in America* (Toronto: Lexington Books, 1991).

Mills, Caroline, "Life on the Upslope," *Society and Space*, vol. 6, 1988.

Murphy, Barbara, *The Ugly Canadian: The Rise and Fall of a Caring Society* (Winnipeg: J. Gordon Shillingford, 1999).

Murphy, J.B.M. et al., "Foster Homes: The New Back Wards?" *Canada's Mental Health*, vol. 20, supplement 71, 1972.

National Council on Welfare, *Poverty Profile 1997* (Ottawa, 1999).

Norris, M.J. and D. Beavon, *Registered Indian Mobility and Migration: An Analysis of 1996 Census Data*, paper presented at the Canadian Population Society meeting, Lennoxville, Quebec, 1999.

Novac, S. et al., *No Room of Her Own: A Literature Review on Women and Homelessness,* Canada Mortgage and Housing (Ottawa, 1996).

Patterson, Ross, "The Development of an Interwar Suburb: Kingsway Park, Etobicoke," *Urban History Review*, vol. 13, February 1985.

Pomeroy, Steve, *Residualization of Rental Tenure: Attitudes of Private Landlords Toward Housing Low-income Households,* Canada Mortgage and Housing (Ottawa, 1998).

Rae, John B., *The American Automobile, A Brief History* (Chicago: University of Chicago Press, 1965).

Richman, Alex, "Long-stay Patients in Canadian Mental Hospitals, 1955-1963," *Canadian Medical Association Journal*, vol. 95, 1966.

Richman, Alex and P. Harris, "Mental Hospital Deinstitutionalization in Canada: A National Perspective with Some Regional Examples," *International Journal of Mental Health*, vol. 11, 1983.

Roberts, C.A. et al., "Psychiatric Services in General Hospitals in Canada: Five Years of Development, 1951-1956," *Canadian Medical Association Journal*, vol. 78, 1958.

Rossi, Peter, *Down and Out in America* (Chicago: University of Chicago Press, 1989).

Rubis, Darryl, *The Changing Character of Ottawa's Golden Triangle: Census Tract 49,* unpublished Master's thesis, Queen's University, 1982.

Schafer, Arthur, *Down and Out in Winnipeg and Toronto: The Ethics of Legislating Against Panhandling,* Caledon Institute of Social Policy (Ottawa, 1998).

Sewell, John, *Houses and Homes, Housing for Canadians* (Toronto: James Lorimer and Co., 1994).

Sewell, John, "The Suburbs," *City Magazine*, vol. 2, January 1977.

Shorter, Edward, ed., *TPH, History and Memories of the Toronto Psychiatric Hospital 1925-1966* (Toronto: Wall and Emerson, 1996).

Simmons, H.G. *Unbalanced, Mental Health Policy in Ontario 1930-1989* (Toronto: Wall and Thompson, 1990).

Skaburskis, A., *The Effect of Development Charges on Urban Formation: An Econometric Analysis,* Canada Mortgage and Housing (Ottawa, 1999).

Smith, Colin M. "Crisis and Aftermath: Community Psychiatry in Saskatchewan 1963-69," *Canadian Psychiatric Association Journal*, vol. 16, 1971.

Smith, Colin M. "From Hospital to Community, A System Changes," *Canadian Journal of Psychiatry*, vol. 24, 1979.

Smith, Colin M. et al., "Care of the Certified Psychiatric Patient in the General Hospital: The Saskatoon Project," *Canadian Medical Association Journal,* vol. 88, 1963.

Smith, Colin M. and D.G. Kerracher, "The Comprehensive Psychiatric Unit in the General Hospital," *American Journal of Psychiatry,* vol. 121, 1964.

Smith, Lawrence, "Economic Implications of Ontario's New Housing Legislation, Bills 11 and 51," *Canadian Public Policy*, XIV, 1988.

Smith, P.J., "Change in a Youthful City: The Case of Calgary, Alberta," *Geography*, vol. 56, 1971.

Splane, Richard, *Social Welfare in Ontario, 1791-1893* (Toronto: University of Toronto Press, 1965).

Steele, Marion, "Conversions, Condominiums, and Capital Gains: The Transformation of the Ontario Rental Housing Market," *Urban Studies*, vol. 30, 1991.

Stelter, Gilbert A. and Alan F.J. Artibise, *The Canadian City: Essays in Urban and Social History* (Ottawa: Carleton University Press, 1984).

Stobie, Peter W., *Private Inner City Redevelopment in Vancouver: A Case Study of Kitsilano*, unpublished Master's thesis, University of British Columbia, 1980.

Sylph, J.A. et al., "Long-term Psychiatric Care in Ontario," *Canadian Medical Association Journal,* vol. 114, 1976.

Taylor, Eva and James Kennedy, *Ottawa's Britannia*, Britannia Historical Association (Ottawa, 1983).

Taylor, John H., *Ottawa, An Illustrated History* (Toronto: James Lorimer and Co., 1986).

Time, "Buddy, Can You Spare a Dime," February 12, 1999.

Tuke, D.H. *The Insane of the United States and Canada* (New York: Arno Press, 1885, reprinted 1973).

Tyhurst, J.S. et al., *More for the Mind, A Study of Psychiatric Services in Canada* (Toronto: Canadian Mental Health Association, 1963).

Ucko, Peter et al, eds., *Man, Settlement and Urbanism* (London: Duckworth, 1972).

U.S. Bureau of the Census, *1990 Census of Population and Housing; Summary Populations and Housing Characteristics* (Washington, 1990).

Weaver, John, "From Land Assembly to Social Maturity: The Suburban Life of Westdale (Hamilton), Ontario, 1911-51," *Social History*, vol. 11, 1978.

Westboro, Ottawa's Westmount, an illustrative number devoted to its past, present and future growth (Ottawa: J. Bower Lyon, June, 1913).

Wilson, Peter J., *The Domestication of the Human Species* (New Haven and London: Yale University Press, 1988).

Newspapers

Calgary Herald

"Man Died of Natural Causes," December 31, 1992.

"Homeless Man Found Dead in East-end Park," January 22, 1999.

"Defiant Panhandlers Vow to Fight Bylaw," March 11, 1999.

Edmonton Journal

Goyette, Linda, "Alberta Slashes Welfare," reprinted in *Ottawa Citizen*, September 9, 1993.

"Coroner's Jury Blames Deaths on Homelessness," July 31, 1996.

Montreal Gazette

"Report on Somalis Cheating Welfare Contains Some Mistakes, Minister Says," November 13, 1993.

"Death Won't Halt Help for City's Needy," December 23, 1997.

"Squeegee Patrols Start," May 16, 1998.

"Man Died After Refusing Shelter," January 21, 2000.

New York Times

"Suit Asserts Right of Homeless to Sleep in Park," August 2, 1992.

"Census Bureau Sued Over Homeless Count," October 11, 1992.

"Homeless Win Access to Beach in Key West," November 30, 1992.

Ottawa Citizen

Calamai, Peter, "Welfare World's Fuzzy Thinking Leaves Loopholes for Abuse," June 15, 1992.

"Briefly," January 6, 1994.

Greenberg, Roger, "The Key to New Housing: Government Must Lower Barriers to Private-Sector Investment," September 6, 1995.

"Customers Come First, Safety Patrol Targets Downtown Nuisances," June 6, 1998.

"Homeless Pregnant Woman Died of Exposure," March 1, 1999.

"Police Have No Clues to Identity of Body Found in Nepean Shed," February 2, 2000.

"I Could Have Been on the Street," February 2, 2000.

Toronto Globe and Mail

"UI Political Trick Up Axworthy's Sleeve," January 19, 1996.

"Social Studies," May 16, 1997.

"Absent Aboriginals," May 24, 1997.

"UN Committee Lambastes Canada on Human Rights," December 5, 1998.

"Just 36% of Jobless Get UI," January 27, 1999.

"UI Changes Hit Youths, Women," March 18, 1999.

Toronto Star

"150 Bid Adieu to Woman Found Frozen," January 9, 1992.

"Welfare Abuse Not Widespread, Report Says," April 19, 1992.

"Be Proud to Take Cut in Payments," December 4, 1992.

Jones, Frank, "Welfare Life is Tough but Food Banks No Answer," June 17, 1993.

"Police Investigate Body in Lot," February 9, 1994.

"Homeless Man Freezes to Death in Bus Shelter," January 6, 1996.

"Another Homeless Man Dies From Cold," February 3, 1996.

"Freezing Victim Died for Nothing," December 3, 1996.

"Body Found Under Bridge," February 4, 1997.

"No Room for Homeless in Purified New York City," December 13, 1998.

"Death of Homeless Man Renews Call to Create More Affordable Housing," February 5, 1999.

Toronto Sun

"Death of Homeless Man Probed," January 27, 1997.

"Did Man Freeze to Death in Garage?" November 21, 1997.

"Bylaw Envy Grips Exasperated City," July 23, 1998.

Vancouver Sun

"Suspicion of UI, Welfare Fraud High," August 25, 1993.

"Surrey's Living Room: Where Homeless Come Out of Cold," December 7, 1994.

"New Westminster Targets Nuisance," May 7, 1998.

Winnipeg Free Press

"Unemployment Officials Crack Down on Fraud," February 26, 1977.

Index